**IMAGE EVALUATION
TEST TARGET (MT-3)**

Photographic
Sciences
Corporation

23 WEST MAIN STREET
WEBSTER, N.Y. 14580
(716) 872-4503

CIHM/ICMH
Microfiche
Series.

CIHM/ICMH
Collection de
microfiches.

Canadian Institute for Historical Microreproductions / Institut canadien de microreproductions historiques

© 1982

Technical and Bibliographic Notes/Notes techniques et bibliographiques

The Institute has attempted to obtain the best original copy available for filming. Features of this copy which may be bibliographically unique, which may alter any of the images in the reproduction, or which may significantly change the usual method of filming, are checked below.

L'Institut a microfilmé le meilleur exemplaire qu'il lui a été possible de se procurer. Les détails de cet exemplaire qui sont peut-être uniques du point de vue bibliographique, qui peuvent modifier une image reproduite, ou qui peuvent exiger une modification dans la méthode normale de filmage sont indiqués ci-dessous.

- [ ] Coloured covers/
  Couverture de couleur

- [ ] Covers damaged/
  Couverture endommagée

- [ ] Covers restored and/or laminated/
  Couverture restaurée et/ou pelliculée

- [ ] Cover title missing/
  Le titre de couverture manque

- [ ] Coloured maps/
  Cartes géographiques en couleur

- [ ] Coloured ink (i.e. other than blue or black)/
  Encre de couleur (i.e. autre que bleue ou noire)

- [ ] Coloured plates and/or illustrations/
  Planches et/ou illustrations en couleur

- [ ] Bound with other material/
  Relié avec d'autres documents

- [ ] Tight binding may cause shadows or distortion along interior margin/
  La re liure serrée peut causer de l'ombre ou de la distortion le long de la marge intérieure

- [ ] Blank leaves added during restoration may appear within the text. Whenever possible, these have been omitted from filming/
  Il se peut que certaines pages blanches ajoutées lors d'une restauration apparaissent dans le texte, mais, lorsque cela était possible, ces pages n'ont pas été filmées.

- [✓] Additional comments:/
  Commentaires supplémentaires:

- [ ] Coloured pages/
  Pages de couleur

- [ ] Pages damaged/
  Pages endommagées

- [ ] Pages restored and/or laminated/
  Pages restaurées et/ou pelliculées

- [✓] Pages discoloured, stained or foxed/
  Pages décolorées, tachetées ou piquées

- [ ] Pages detached/
  Pages détachées

- [✓] Showthrough/
  Transparence

- [ ] Quality of print varies/
  Qualité inégale de l'impression

- [ ] Includes supplementary material/
  Comprend du matériel supplémentaire

- [ ] Only edition available/
  Seule édition disponible

- [ ] Pages wholly or partially obscured by errata slips, tissues, etc., have been refilmed to ensure the best possible image/
  Les pages totalement ou partiellement obscurcies par un feuillet d'errata, une pelure, etc., ont été filmées à nouveau de façon à obtenir la meilleure image possible.

This item is filmed at the reduction ratio checked below/
Ce document est filmé au taux de réduction indiqué ci-dessous.

10X		14X		18X		22X		26X		30X	
		✓									
	12X		16X		20X		24X		28X		32X

...CE OF PLACES.

QUEBEC TO BYTOWN.

	Miles.	Miles.
Montreal,	—	180
St. Eustache,	21	201
St. Andrews,	24	225
Chatham,	3	228
Grenville,	12	240
Petite Nation,	30	270
Bytown,	33	303
Kingston, through the Rideau Canal,	135	438

EASTERN TOWNSHIPS.
FROM QUEBEC.

	Miles.	Miles.
St. Nicholas,	—	6
Leeds,	27	33
Ireland,	17	50
Dudswell,	35	85
Eaton,	20	105
Clifton,	10	115
Hereford,	17	132

ROUTE TO STANSTEAD, &c.

	Miles.	Miles.
Dudswell as above,	—	85
Lennoxville,	17	102
Sherbrooke,	3	105
Stanstead,	34	137

... TO QUEBEC.

	Miles.	Miles.
La Prairie,	18	377
Montreal,	9	386
Quebec,	180	566

THE
EMIGRANT'S GUIDE,

OR

CANADA AS IT IS.

COMPRISING DETAILS RELATING

TO THE

DOMESTIC POLICY, COMMERCE AND AGRICULTURE,

OF THE

UPPER AND LOWER PROVINCES,

COMPRISING MATTER OF GENERAL INFORMATION AND INTEREST, ESPECIALLY INTENDED FOR THE USE OF SETTLERS AND EMIGRANTS.

BY GEORGE HENRY.

QUEBEC,
PUBLISHED BY WILLIAM GRAY & Co.
BUADE STREET,
And sold by all Booksellers.

TABLE OF DISTAN(

QUEBEC TO TORONTO, &c.

	Miles.	Miles.
Quebec to Montreal,	—	180
Montreal to Lachine, by Canal,	9	189
Lachine to Cascades, towed by Steamer,	24	213
Cascades to Côteau du Lac, tracked by Horses,	16	229
Côteau du Lac to Cornwall, towed by Steamer,	41	270
Cornwall to Prescott, tracked by Horses,	50	320
Prescott to Brockville, by Steamer,	12	332
Brockville to Kingston, by Steamer,	60	392
Kingston to Cobourg, by Steamer,	120	512
Cobourg to Port Hope, by Steamer,	7	519
Port Hope to Toronto, (late York,) by Steamer.	63	582
	402	582

QUEBEC ENVIRONS.

	Miles.	Miles.
Quebec to Falls of Montmorency,	9	
do. Ditto of Chaudière,	11	
do. Indian Village of Lorette,	9	
do. Fishing Lake at Beauport.	10	

FROM NEW YORK

	Miles.	Miles.
Albany,	—	140
Whitehall,	69	209
St. John's, L. C. by Lake Champlain,	150	359

DISTANCE OF PLACES.

QUEBEC TO BYTOWN.

	Miles.	Miles.		Miles.	Miles.
, &c.		180	Montreal,	—	180
			St. Eustache,	21	201
	9	189	St. Andrews,	24	225
			Chatham,	3	228
	24	213	Grenville,	12	240
			Petite Nation,	30	270
ies,	16	229	Bytown,	33	303
			Kingston, through the Rideau Canal,	135	438
ier,	41	270			

EASTERN TOWNSHIPS.
FROM QUEBEC.

	50	320		Miles.	Miles.
	12	332	St. Nicholas,	—	6
	60	392	Leeds,	27	33
			Ireland,	17	50
	120	512	Dudswell,	35	85
	7	519	Eaton,	20	105
			Clifton,	10	115
ier.	63	582	Hereford,	17	132
	402	582			

ROUTE TO STANSTEAD, &c.

	Miles.	Miles.		Miles.	Miles.
	9		Dudswell as above,	—	85
	11		Lennoxville,	17	102
	9		Sherbrooke,	3	105
	10		Stanstead,	34	137

EW YORK TO QUEBEC.

	Miles.	Miles.		Miles.	Miles.
	—	140	La Prairie,	18	377
	69	209	Montreal,	9	386
	150	359	Quebec,	180	566

RARE
FC
41
H3

CANAD
or agricult
mands bo
are fast ri
care of th
in the W
the attent
The G
times acc
for inlan
rence, pu
real, a dis
presents
similar ex
that allo
land seas
lending t
municati
QUEF
British
Nature a
St. Law
traction
ed, from
Rock, o

PREFACE.

Canada, whether considered in her political, commercial or agricultural relations, has attained an elevation that commands both respect and attention: her growing energies are fast ripening to a maturity, that aided by the fostering care of the Mother Country, will establish her importance in the Western Hemisphere, and enable her to command the attention of the world.

The Geographical situation of Canada renders her at all times accessible to the ships of England whilst her resources for inland navigation are unrivalled. The noble St. Lawrence, pursues a navigable course from the Gulf to Montreal, a distance of nearly five hundred miles : Lake Ontario presents a surface equal to that of Ireland : Erie is of a similar extent, whilst Huron occupies a space as large as that allotted to the British Isles. These magnificent inland seas form the natural barrier to the upper province, lending their waters to her inhabitants as the means of communication and commercial enterprize.

QUEBEC, the remarkable fortress and boast of the British Crown, in America, rendered impregnable by Nature and Art, challenges the regard of the voyager up the St. Lawrance, nor does his nearer approach lessen the attraction ; from whatever point the Fortifications are viewed, from the plains of Abraham, from Beauport, from St. Rock, or from Point Levi, the highest admiration must be excited, by their beauty and grandeur. In the summer the prospect from the Citadel is beautiful in the extreme; let us suppose a height of from four to five hundred feet commanding a view of the Noble Stream that waters its base, for an immense distance; its bosom covered with vessels, some stretching their course to the ocean, others entering the port, the wharves crowded by individuals engaged in loading or unloading their respective cargoes; whilst the hum of industry arising above them, and the cheerful and well known chorus as each stick of timber finds its level, adds new life to the scene: here may we behold hundreds of Emigrants already busied in their newly adopted Country, in securing their little properties; how readily may they be reconized, by the astonished gaze at the surrounding objects, and by the anxious inquiry how to proceed towards the place of their destination; they contribute to the illusion of the picture, and render Quebec at this season of the year a city of the utmost interest and variety.

The timber trade of Quebec either as connected with the interior of the country by the employment of labourers, or as supplying cargoes for a thousand or twelve hundred vessels, is entitled to the most serious consideration of the Government at home: that one port should be able to freight upwards of a thousand ships, in bona fide British bottoms, by the means of British capital, and what is of infinitely higher importance, through the aid of British subjects, is no less cheering than astonishing. In addition to the commercial advantages thus realized, how important is the encouragement of such a trade with reference to the hardy race it supports—the timber trade of Quebec, may be considered as a nursery for seamen, that valuable class to whom the whole Empire of Britain is so much indebted both in prosecution of the duties of war, and the arts of peace it also assists in the support of another class of men, whose services are scarcely less essential, the Raftsmen or Shantcemen—but the advantages of the trade are prodigious in other points of view; hundreds and thousands of poor Emigrants who are of little value at home, are transported by means of these ships to a situation, where their exertions largely contribute to the national prosperity; an incredible number of families with scarcely a six pence in the world are nevertheless enabled to reach the western Continent by means of the timber ships, and are at once rescued from misery and poverty by the adaptation of their labour to the wants of the country. Ireland is relieved of some portion of her excessive population, who are too often goaded on by want to the commission of the most atrocious crimes, and Canada receives a useful and industrious race, who can be rendered faithful citizens by the simple remedy of employment; thus these ships, and the country at large, may be regarded almost as in the light of a safety valve to unhappy Ireland, in relieving her at least from a portion of the pressure, which every instant threatens an explosion.

Should not these combined considerations, then, arrest the attention of the British Legislation, ere they pass an act (the non-protection act,) that would blight the prospects of thousands, throw a damp over the whole of these provinces, and nip in the very bud of their prosperity, the most interesting and rising Colonies attached to the Empire.

If it be the intention of England to retain the Canadas as colonies, a lukewarm policy will scarcely effect her purpose; a neighboring power has already cast a jealous eye on this northern territory, and would gladly seize a favorable opportunity for attaching it to her sway; for with this possession America might bid defiance to Europe. Such an union can, however, never take place, so long as a liberal policy

PREFACE.

is adopted towards the Canadians; identified from motives of interest and from long association with the principles that govern the mother country, they are cheerfully devoted to her sovereignty, notwithstanding the anti-British feelings that have emanated from a certain class of the community of England, as much opposed to the national welfare generally, as to the prosperity of the Canadas in particular.—The last war produced numerous examples of Colonial attachment to the ancient home; the battles of England were fought by Canadians, who displayed the utmost heroism, more especially in an action fought near Lake Champlain, under the late gallant Colonel de la Saleberry, which we select as the best illustration of their bravery and patriotism: not that this was a single example, for the whole campaign teemed with proofs that the Canadians of the Upper Province were essentially British in character and feeling.

A period has arrived when the necessity of protection to these colonies can no longer be denied; their claims are of paramount importance not only to themselves, but to England. If we regard the internal policy of other countries, what do we behold? On this continent, our indefatigable neighbours are striving in the race with their former parent; in manufactures of almost every fabric they are contending, if not for the mastership, at least for an equality. Birminghams and Manchesters have started into existence, and the success of their youthful efforts guarantees the future results; already they compete not only in number, in proportion to the population of the country, but in quality with the manufactures that boast a century's endurance. In the town of Paterson, in the state of New-Jersey, thirty-six cotton manufactories are in active operation, and the prosperity of this town is rivalled by that of several others in the different sections of the Union.

In Russia also a successful experiment has been made to supply her population from domestic manufactures; the artisans of France and Germany excel in some fabrics, and are rapidly improving in others, and already are the European markets preparing to exclude the produce of English labour;—these considerations are surely sufficient to awaken attention to the rising condition of Canada, where an increased demand for home manufactures will be created in proportion to the increased settlement of the country; when other markets fail, the supply to these colonies will atone for the deficiency, and thus every advantage that can be now afforded them by England, will ultimately be repaid in a tenfold degree.

The public works in Canada are on the point of accomplishing their promised benefits;—the Rideau canal, in particular, which, under the superintendance of the able and indefatigable Lieut. Colonel J. By, is on the eve of completion, as the locks, which are admirable specimens of masonry, are all finished, and steam-boats and other craft have already commenced their passages between Kingston and Bytown. This magnificent undertaking, which may be designated as the great channel of Canadian prosperity, as one of the principal links in that vast chain of inland navigation extending from New-Orleans to Quebec, planned with so much ingenuity and executed with so much skill, is of no less importance in a commercial and political light, than as a means of opening and improving the country in its track. The design that reflects immortal credit upon its proposers, when completely realized, will indeed serve to contradict the assertion of an Honourable Member of the Commons House of Parliament during the last session,

A4

"that it would be better to forego the Rideau canal altogether, and sacrifice the monies already expended on that work than to vote any further sums for the completion of the undertaking." The absurdity of this remark renders its contradiction needless, especially as it could only be made by one who was totally ignorant of the local bearings of the country.

Bytown, so named after its distinguished founder, is situate at the mouth of the canal, and affords tolerable evidence of the usefulness of this truly national work; but five years ago, its site was an absolute wilderness—now a bustling and lively town occupies the soil so lately covered by the forest. Three thousand inhabitants, comprising English, Scotch, Irish, Canadians and Americans, have here found a home, an Episcopalian, a Roman Catholic, and a Methodist church, and a Scotch kirk, have been erected for their worship; there are numerous and excellent stores provided with all the varied produce and manufactures of the world, for the supply of their necessities, whilst the general appearance of the town, ornamented with several handsome stone houses, proclaims its rapid and almost daily improvement. In proceeding up the line of the canal, the change effected on the rugged face of nature is no less pleasing than surprising; the vast interior is opened to the industry of man; the landscape, dotted here and there with snug farms and comfortable dwellings, is relieved from its former monotony, and the addition of a good tavern to the scene, adds to the traveller's and the neighbour's enjoyment. For forty miles above Bytown this appearance is presented; the canal has indeed fertilized the country! In its passage through the centre of the Rideau settlement the same wondrous improvement is visible; houses, mills, stores, and buildings of every description, and bridges over the canal

PREFACE. ix

that has accomplished all these benefits, testify how much has already been done in the profitable settlement of the country.

About five miles above the settlement of Rideau, and immediately on the line of the canal, is situated the village of Merricksville, which has sprung up with astonishing quickness into a place of considerable consequence; two years ago the spot now covered with well-built dwellings, was a solitary wilderness; a little market town is established in the forest land, and stores, mills, and taverns are seen on every side. Mechanics of all grades have flocked to the infant settlement, which is thus provided with every necessary establishment.

The salutary effects accruing from the opening of the Rideau canal, are not however confined to the immediate vicinity of its course; the communicating advantages are and will be experienced through the surrounding country. Perth, for instance, a neighboring town and settlement of some standing and consequence, will reap immense benefit; it is intended to render the river Tay, running a distance of eight miles from that place to the Rideau, a navigable stream by the subscription of the inhabitants of the town and its neighbourhood, under the immediate auspices of Mr. William Morris, of Perth, the highly respected member for the county of Lanark. Passing onwards from Merricksville on the line of the Rideau to Kingston, the same decided improvement is apparent as elsewhere,—in fact, throughout the whole length of country traversed by the canal, the results of intelligence and industry have succeeded to the wildness and desolation of the waste.

Should then the completion of this work, that in its progress has been so productive of usefulness to the infant settlements on its margin, be abandoned, the prospects of

A5

PREFACE.

thousands of emigrants will be blasted, the hopes they have been led to form from previous prosperity, defeated, and the efforts that have already accomplished so much in the improvements of their condition, paralized.

The encouragement of public works in Canada provides the emigrant with immediate employment, if circumstances prevent his early establishment, and indeed the knowledge of such undertakings induces numerous bands of labourers to seek the country with no other object in view than to engage in them. The importance of this class of emigrants to society will be admitted by all who recollect the scarcity and dearness of labour during the last summer, when in many of the townships above York,—Markham, Vaughan, King, Whitchurch, Georgina, and others, a dollar a day, and in some instances, six shillings currency, were paid in addition to the board of the laborer.

The privilege granted to Canada by the Government, of the admission of her grain into British ports, under a very low duty, has wrought a surprising change in the habits of the farmers; the land was formerly tilled merely for the support of his family, for he had no market to relieve him from a surplus produce; Sumac, the Raspberry, and other woods were permitted to grow in the place of corn, and the time of the farmer was occupied in shooting or fishing, from the imposibility of employing it to a useful purpose in agricultural pursuit. At the present time he obtains a fair and remunerating price for all the grain he can raise, and the farm is therefore in good order and continually improving in value; he is enabled to pay excellent wages to a numerous band of laborers, to clothe his family in British fabrics, and thus in the advancement of his own prosperity to reciprocate the advantages afforded to him by the mother country.

During the last season there arrived at Quebec, about 49,000 emigrants, the majority of whom were laborers, who distributed themselves in the districts of the upper province; still the effect of this increase is imperceptible. In the northern settlements bordering on the Ottawa, in the Midland districts above and below Kingston, in the interior settled parts towards York, on Yonge Street, Newmarket, Lake Simcoe, Dundas Street, Dundas, Hamilton, Niagara, the London district, and all the large settlements on the shores of Lake Erie, the addition of numbers has scarcely been felt, and in fact had three times the quantum of emigration occurred in this province, the supply would scarcely have been recognized on the face of the country.

It has been calculated that the number of emigrants to Quebec this season, will amount to 80,000, and certainly the last reports from England justify the assumption. The prejudice in favor of the United States is declining very fast in England, and every year will witness a larger arrival into these provinces; the tide of British emigration sets towards Canada, bearing the hardy sons of England Scotland and Ireland from countries too densely peopled to allow the display of their strength, to a soil sufficiently extensive for its perfect development, and abundantly fertile to reward their exertions.

Of late years, a number of the middle classes of British society have settled in these provinces, in addition to the class of poor settlers. Voltaire in speaking of the component parts of the British community, observes, that they may be justly compared to their favourite beverage "beer"; the top or the higher orders, is all froth, the bottom, or the poorer class all dregs, but the middle, excellent: this is an overcharged picture, but not altogether without its likeness, and from this excellent middle portion of soci-

PREFACE.

ety, comprising so much virtuous principle, moral order, and superior intelligence, the Canadas have obtained, and will yet acquire in a larger proportion than heretofore, many families and individuals who contribute so much to the well-being and advancement of the country of their adoption.

Montreal, the leading town of Canada, is foremost in the march of improvement; her new streets laid out with the utmost neatness and regularity, the excellent houses that adorn the suburbs, the convenient wharves, and to crown the whole, that splendid edifice, the new Catholic church in the centre of the city, which may be regarded with equal pride and admiration, as the noblest temple of North America, are all evidences that the spirit of the times has travelled in this direction. But, this spirit is not only recognized in the town; if we visit the neighbourhood, we witness an agricultural system in full operation, that must commend it to the notice of the British farmer; the farms are in a state of the highest cultivation, the regular plan of successive tillage adopted in England, is here acted upon, and the results as may rationally be supposed are no less encouraging. The establishment of agricultural societies in the vicinity of Montreal, has been productive of the utmost service to the agricultural interest; the popular errors which were persevered in, simply because they had been transmitted from a past to a present generation, the prejudices retained by ignorance, or the caprices dictated by folly, have yielded to the spirit of modern discoveries; the farmers of the upper provinces and particularly those in the vicinity of Montreal, have adopted the provisions of an English system in the cultivation of the soil, and they need only ask comparison with the agriculturlists of Lower Canada, to prove their infinite superiority. It is a subject of regret that the Canadians of the lower province are still characterized by their former apathy and indifference to improvements, notwithstanding the prosperous condition of their neighbours; but the time will surely arrive when a common interest will inspire common exertions in every part of this territory, capable of producing equal benefits throughout its whole extent. In the different cities and towns, individuals are to be found in the exercise of their respective vocations, who would confer credit upon any European society: the professions are filled by men of character and learning; the commercial interests are promoted by Merchants of intelligence and respectability; the trading classes and the Mechanics lend their means and their industry to the general weal, so that the increasing population of this comparatively new country are in possession of nearly all the advantages enjoyed by the oldest community. A general confidence is experienced in the respective exertions of each other; an indulgence is extended to the efforts of the humblest individual; a reciprocal interchange of commodities takes place from the manufactured article, to the animal or vegetable product; the effects of a well regulated society are recognized in the arrangements which provide for the education of the young, the restraint of disorderly habits, so common in a new settlement, and an obedience to the laws and the encouragement of industry:—such are the pleasing results attendant upon the prosperity of the Canadas.

There are few circumstances that have contributed so much to the condition we have described, as steam navigation; the facilities afforded by the lakes and rivers for personal conveyance, and the transport of merchandize and the products of the soil have been eagerly accepted; the freight of goods by steam vessels to York, during the last season amounted to between nine and ten thousand pounds, multitudes of emigrants have been conveyed to their place of destination, and the staples of the numerous Merchants and farmers in the interior have thus been readily transmitted to a market.

The Banks likewise, especially those of Montreal and York, have in the mode in which they are conducted, proved of incalculable usefulness. The discounts are not only liberal as commensurate with the security, but the returns of payment are so arranged as materially to increase the value of the accommodation: for instance; a note of one hundred pounds is discounted at ninety days date; at the expiration of that time one fourth of the amount is only required in payment, renewing the note for the balance for an additional ninety days; another twenty five pounds is then paid, with a similar renewal; a third takes place for the remainder of the time, and the last payment is discharged at the end of another ninety days when the original advance is liquidated. All these renewals are of course granted at the common rate of interest, and without the expense of stamps, and by this means the time of a twelvemonth is allowed for the complete payment of the loan. There is one fact connected with the York Bank that strikingly illustrates the present healthy state of commerce in the upper province; when it was first established, a charter was offered, limiting the subscribed capital to two hundred thousand pounds; this extensive limit was at the time properly declined by the Directors, on account of the infant state of the Colony, which rendered the profitable employment of so large a sum very precarious, and would therefore have returned but a small interest to the proprietors, at the same time depreciating the value of the stock in public estimation; a charter was therefore accepted for a bank with one hundred thousand pounds capital. This occurred but a few years ago; during the last session of the House of Assembly an application was made and complied with for the extension of the capital to the original proposed amount, as the Directors found that the increasing demands of the commercial and other interests required an enlargment of their accustomed issues.

In the following description of the Canadas, it is the intention of the author to convey such information to the emigrant as will assist him in his progress; the details are founded on practical experience, and may fairly be contrasted with many of the garbled and interested statements that have proved injurious to the settler. The individual who seeks the Canadas for a home, has much to learn; a previous knowledge of the current affairs of life will serve him but little in a new country, where the habits, the practical operations of handicraft, the applicability of science, the mode of trade, and the pursuits of agriculture are foreign to his former experience; he is introduced upon a scene where he is opposed by strange and unforeseen exigencies which must be surmounted ere he can pursue his course; his steps are impeded by difficulties which must be removed before he can track the route leading to his future independence. An emigrant blessed with strength and hardihood, and being moreover in the prime of life, will not consult his permanent interest by embarking his fortunes in an old settlement; a country untouched by the hand of man is before him, clothed in a native verdure, and portioned with a native fertility—let him strip the forest of her gigantic mantle, convert the wilderness into the fruitful plain, and force the treasures from the bosom of nature. The virgin soil will repay the exertions of man by an abundant increase, and the proud reflection will be enjoyed of having carved out from a mass of incongruous materials, the means of future

xvi   PREFACE.

support and comfort. There will be inconveniences and privations, but let them be endured; they cannot resist continued exertions, and man will in the end become the conqueror. The settler must rise with the lark in his daily career; he must be early in the field, for afternoon farming will not serve his purpose, and this is true not only in the commencement of his undertaking, or as applied to his daily labor, but in reference to the culture of his land; for it is an admitted fact, that in this country late crops seldom reward the agriculturist, while early field labor is almost invariably crowned with success.

The emigrant who possesses sufficient means for his support for sometime after his arrival in the country should pause ere he determines the place of his settlement; the few extra pounds expended in the survey of the different locations will purchase the most valuable information, and render him equal to the task of choosing for himself, instead of acting upon the interested counsel of others. In traversing the country, let him visit the various settlements already established, regard the conveniences or the objections to their situation, and penetrate into the *bush*, to ascertain the capabilities of improvement there presented: he can learn little on the deck of a steam-boat, or by a continuance in the towns, beyond the common-place instructions that are of trifling benefit. No! he must dive beneath the surface into the recesses of the country, to witness the enterprising and persevering exertions of others, to discover the gradual development of power in overcoming the mighty obstacles that oppose the emigrant, and to gain a knowledge of the means that have elevated Canada to her present prosperous condition.

In a few years, the whole territory of the Canada, must exhibit the appearances now presented in some of the dis-

PREFACE. xvii

tricts; the desert and the forest will have disappeared under emigrant labor, to give place to thriving and populous towns; trade and commerce, progressing in the ratio in which they have hitherto advanced, will have increased to an infinite extent; and a crowded and intelligent population will reap the fruits of former toil. The main channel of Canadian prosperity is unquestionably her water communication; her inland seas, the vast lakes of the American Continent, and the river St. Lawrence have already been alluded to, but hardly in terms of sufficient praise; no country in the world can boast a similar extent of lake navigation, and in no country can be discovered a stream of greater beauty and usefulness; whether we regard the St. Lawrence, the grand boundary stream, as a natural defence in war, or as the great channel of Commerce in peace, it is equally entitled to our admiration; the advantages it affords in each respect can only be estimated by the consequences that are every where apparent, in the increasing wealth of the country, and the happiness of its inhabitants; in the metamorphosis of a desert into a thriving and populous state.

The exclusive right of British subjects to the navigation of this river, has an important reference both to the political power, and the trading privileges of the Provinces; to share this privilege would be to anticipate the eventual loss of the Canadas, for in the first place the carrying trade to the British shipping would be engrossed by others, and the facilities of smuggling be increased; and in the second the interests of two separate powers would so often clash in the prosecution of a mutual privilege, as to be productive of the utmost confusion, and finally terminate in the anihilation of Colonial prosperity. It is however almost impossible to imagine the commital of such an act of folly, notwithstanding the plausible arguments of our Commercial opponents, for although it were admitted at the present period that the expanse of navigable waters in Canada affords ample range for the shipping of both countries, it may be reasonably surmised that ere the lapse of many years, the British and native tonnage will be doubled or trebled in the Colonial trade, and that the St. Lawrence will become the Baltic of America through the exercise of the protected energies of these Provinces.

The wealth of every country consists in a surplus product beyond the necessities of consumption, whether through the agency of the husbandman or the manufacturer; Canada is already capable of raising an immense surplus, and is therefore in the possession of immense wealth—with her present limited means of cultivation, her great staple, wheat, forms an article of profitable export, and there can be no doubt that if the country were brought to its proper bearing, and the surface adapted to its legitimate purpose throughout its extent, a supply of grain could be raised capable of relieving the severest necessities of the mother country, and rendering her independent of a foreign state for the food of her inhabitants. But, there are prospective as well as actual advantages; in the article of hemp, an admirable opportunity is offered of rendering England dependent upon her colonies rather than a stranger; the very best quality might readily be grown in Canada, as much to the advantage of the grower, as of importance to the merchant, in the improvement of the soil on the one hand, and the encouragement of trade on the other. These are sufficient examples, although others might be named, of the actual and possible resources of this territory; extent of surface, fertility of soil, goodness of climate, and an increase in population are the assistants to her prosperity, and the ability of the exporting such an amount of native produce as will pay for the imported articles, must ere many years, have witnessed the exertions of the population, place her on the same level with the most favoured countries.

The great misfortune of England is her excessive population, over a small tract of Country; the draw back upon Canada, is the want of a sufficient number of inhabitants—thus the interests of both countries are served by emigration; the former parts with that, which is a burden upon her soil, whilst the latter receives the only gift that can render her soil of advantage. Important as emigration is to Canada, it is yet of more consequence to the poor of Britain; the frequent accounts of their abject misery, of the wretched poverty that too often drives them to the commission of crimes, are sufficient inducements to the philanthropist to promote their removal from the scene of distress; an opportunity is afforded them, upon the cheapest terms that a benefit was ever proposed, of exchangeing beggary for independence, starvation for plenty, idleness and disease, for health and exertion: they effect a beneficial alteration in their own circumstances, and at the same time lend important aid to the society in which they are received. It is not desirable that all emigrants should be in affluent circumstances; the duty required at their hands is varied in its kind, from the labours in the study, the office, and the laboratory, to those at the loom, in the field, and in public works; there is occupation for all, employment in every description of trade and handicraft. The poorest individuals are rendered valuable assistants to the general community, and there are repeated instances of families who upon their arrival did not possess the means to purchase the next meal, having attained to a condition of decent competency. If such individuals had remained at home, how different their lot! doomed to suffer poverty and want, to eke out a miserable existence by subsisting upon the charity of the benevolent, they would have 'lived as miserable dependents, and oppressed society still further by entailing a needy offspring upon its members; as emigrants, on the contrary, the opportunity for bodily and mental improvement is offered to them; they have no excuse for refusing it, and in the majority of instances the force of example operates as a spur in its ready acceptance; they work and their labour is rewarded, they earn more than is required for their wants, they save money, purchase property, become lords of the soil, and hold a stake in the advancing prosperity of the country.

As yet, the population of the Canadas is trifling in comparison to its extent; notwithstanding the length of time they have been attached to the crown, and the number of emigrants who have arrived, vast tracts are untenanted; hitherto a large number of families who had left the English shores for the American continent, travelled through Canada to the United States, or embarked for ports in that country, in consequence of the encouragement they received to settle in N. York, Pensylvania Ohio &c., an encouragement which was was denied to them by their own government; latterly the system has been happily changed, protection has been extended to the emigrants in the British provinces, and, as might have been expected, Canada receives by far the larger portion; thousands of subjects are thus retained in their allegiance, British property is rendered more valuable by their assistance, and the national welfare is promoted by their instrumentality, at the same time that their own social enjoyment is secured in all the relations and comforts of existence.

The settlement of some individuals in the Canadas, possessing a considerable capital, is unquestionably an object of much interest and importance; the value of the money introduced into the country in directing labour, and in accomplishing under one design great measures of improvement, is no less experienced than the benefit afforded to society at large, in the example displayed by their conduct and behavior; they in fact check the growth of rudeness and vulgarity,—they are the promoters of education, which bears as strongly upon the moral as the intellectual condition of the population, and they keep up and regulate that social order in the community, and if we may so express it, that tone in Canadian society that adds to the convenience and the happiness of all.

The subject of emigration is an important one, and it would be singular if it possessed not its opponents as well as its advocates; so often, indeed, have these met in argument, that the topic may be said to have been sufficiently examined for the discovery of its merits and defects. We have already alluded to the past and present condition of the Canadas, and urged the absolute necessity of a large population, if it be intended to relieve the mother country from the burthen of supporting them; their soil is waiting for the labourer, their natural advantages are ready for acceptance, the thick forest requires but the industry of man to convert it into the fertile field. What the United States have done, that can the Canadas perform, but only through the same means—an immense increase of population.

There are no arguments that can weaken the importance of these facts as they apply to this territory. As far as regards emigration from the British Isles, it has been asserted, that if all the means of employment were duly appropriated in those situations, there would no longer be any necessity for the settlement of their inhabitants in distant lands;—this sounds well, but the theory alone exists; if we could remodel society, or engraft some new elements into its composition, a new order of circumstances might arise, and arrangements that suited with every class of society be accomplished; but, in the mean time, what remedy can be proposed for the relief of the abject and starving thousands, who convert once merry England into a scene of the deepest distress,—who fill the prisons in Ireland, and groan under the miseries of poverty in Scotland? They are unassisted by ingenious theories, and unaided by arguments of what ought to be done;—the hungry are not fed, nor the naked clothed by such philanthropy. The evils endured are evident beyond contradiction; and the only mode by which they can be lessened, is *emigration*, which gives to tens of thousands the means of support, and the comfortable home denied them in the land of their birth. Let the authorities, then, in the various parishes of Britain, whose inhabitants are taxed almost beyond endurance for the support of their poor, contribute in the formation of a fund, that in its application shall relieve their complaint; the remedy is in their own hands, and consists simply in providing each applicant with the means of transport to Canada, and a small sum in his hands when he arrives at Quebec: thus will they get rid of incumbrances upon their own property, and at the same time afford the fairest means in promoting the happiness of their fellow-beings. The partial relief extended to paupers, who express an inclination to proceed to the western continent is a most improvident application of funds; the trifling sum yielded is barely sufficient to pay their expenses to the nearest sea-port,—and thus they are thrown upon another portion of society with the same wants as before. Give to the emigrant sufficient to pay his passage, and support him for a short time after arrival in his new country, and if he possess the moral or physical ability of improvement, he must succeed in working out his own

PREFACE. xxiii

independence, and will probably gain all the comforts of existence. The present lot of these individuals whose parents settled in Canada, is an admirable illustration of these remarks; they are in the possession of excellent farms, of large and profitable tracts of land, they hold a most important stake in the prosperity of the country, and rank with the most useful members of the community; how were these advantages procured? By the very exertions now required at the hands of the emigrants; they were the same race of people as the present, distinguished by the same character, depressed by similar misfortunes at home, poor but hardy, destitute of means, or very nearly so, upon their arrival, but determined to persevere in overcoming the first obstacles, and laying the foundation of future benefits.

In reviewing, then, the previous considerations, it appears that there are three prevailing circumstances in favor of emigration to these colonies; firstly, the comparative short distance from Britain, as under the present improvement in navigation, the voyage is accomplished at the average rate of thirty days; secondly, the extreme healthiness of the climate, as proved by the condition of the population; and thirdly, the facilities presented for immediate employment, by which the necessities of the settler are provided for.

If it be said with respect to the healthiness of the climate, that the assumption is contradicted by the prevalence of swamps in some districts, the objection is easily resisted;—granted that the swamp land is unwholesome, how long, let it be asked, can this continue? Until the country is supplied in all its parts with a population, who will drain these swamps, and render them the finest meadow land in the world. Canada is not singular in this respect; nearly every country in its infancy has been subjected to diseases arising from collections of stagnant air and water; but directly the industry of man has cleared the forest, and drained the swamp, the sources of those diseases have been dried up, and a pure atmosphere reigns in the place of the miasm that heretofore prevailed. In those districts, where settlements have been formed, no complaints of this nature can be entertained, and in proportion as the country is redeemed from the waste by successive bands of emigrants, the swamps and the sickness they occasion will disappear, whilst fertile meadows and a healthy people will proclaim the change that has been effected in the face of nature.

It only remains for England duly to appreciate the natural advantages of the Canadas, and to act towards them with a liberal and enlightened policy that shall not only improve their domestic welfare, and add to the happiness of thousands who seek them as a home, but that shall increase their rising national importance as connected with the mother country, and render them willing assistants in the exchange of commercial friendship, and powerful auxiliaries in circumstances of difficulty, whenever they may occur. The germs of future greatness are sown, and will ripen and bear fruit in due season, provided a parent's hand will protect their infancy.

The shops are spacious and plentifully stocked with goods, some of which will suprise the new-comer by their apparent cheapness ; for, instance, he may purchase brandy at seven shillings a gallon, rum at six, and whiskey at two and sixpence ; and the very cheapness of these articles has too often been the means of destruction to the settler. On the opposite bank of the St. Lawrence stands the picturesque village of Point Levi, in which are erected many comfortable villas, and the country around the city is well cultivated by some of the old country farmers, who display the knowledge of a superior system of agriculture.

About ten miles from Quebec, is the interesting village of Indian Lorette, consisting of about one hundred houses, and principally inhabited by Indians of the Huron tribe, with a slight mixture of Canadians. The four chiefs who visited England a few years ago, reside in this place, in very neat and clean wooden houses : they all possess some relics of their visit, hung up in the most conspicuous parts of their dwellings, and appear to set much value on an excellent engraved portrait of his late Majesty George the Fourth. John Vincent, the principal Chief, and who is also styled king of Lorette, has, in addition to the portraits, two medals, one gold, and the other silver, of con-

4   CANADA AS IT IS.

siderable value, which the king personally presented to him.* There are two extremely neat and clean Catholic churches in the village, one for the Indians' and the other for the Canadians' worship; the former is handsomely decorated with an abundance of images, and the roof bespangled with gilded dots, and is regularly attended by a devout congregation. These Indians, and others of their tribe, receive annual presents from the British Government, as equivalents for their conceded territories.

The passage from Quebec to Montreal is pleasant, particularly in fine weather; the accommoda-

---

* In a visit paid to this village by the author and a party of his friends, the utmost hospitality was exercised towards them; his Majesty was not at home upon their arrival, but the Queen, a good looking Squaw, did the honours and received them very cordially, presenting cakes, maple syrup &c., for their refreshment. Her Majesty with her daughters were busily employed in making fancy baskets for sale, and observed, that she was obliged to work, but that the Queen of England was both paid and kept. In a short time the King returned home, with a rush basket suspended from his neck, containing a hare and some wild fowl, the produce of his day's sport: he was a tall good looking man, about fifty years of age; was very courteous to his visitors and appeared exceedingly kind and attentive to his wife and family, who evidently regarded him with much respect.

The shops are spacious and plentifully stocked with goods, some of which will suprise the new-comer by their apparent cheapness; for, instance, he may purchase brandy at seven shillings a gallon, rum at six, and whiskey at two and sixpence; and the very cheapness of these articles has too often been the means of destruction to the settler. On the opposite bank of the St. Lawrence stands the picturesque village of Point Levi, in which are erected many comfortable villas, and the country around the city is well cultivated by some of the old country farmers, who display the knowledge of a superior system of agriculture.

About ten miles from Quebec, is the interesting village of Indian Lorette, consisting of about one hundred houses, and principally inhabited by Indians of the Huron tribe, with a slight mixture of Canadians. The four chiefs who visited England a few years ago, reside in this place, in very neat and clean wooden houses: they all possess some relics of their visit, hung up in the most conspicuous parts of their dwellings, and appear to set much value on an excellent engraved portrait of his late Majesty George the Fourth. John Vincent, the principal Chief, and who is also styled king of Lorette, has, in addition to the portraits, two medals, one gold, and the other silver, of considerable value, which the king personally presented to him.* There are two extremely neat and clean Catholic churches in the village, one for the Indians' and the other for the Canadians' worship; the former is handsomely decorated with an abundance of images, and the roof bespangled with gilded dots, and is regularly attended by a devout congregation. These Indians, and others of their tribe, receive annual presents from the British Government, as equivalents for their conceded territories.

The passage from Quebec to Montreal is pleasant, particularly in fine weather; the accommoda-

---

* In a visit paid to this village by the author and a party of his friends, the utmost hospitality was exercised towards them; his Majesty was not at home upon their arrival, but the Queen, a good looking Squaw, did the honours and received them very cordially, presenting cakes, maple syrup &c., for their refreshment. Her Majesty with her daughters were busily employed in making fancy baskets for sale, and observed, that she was obliged to work, but that the Queen of England was both paid and kept. In a short time the King returned home, with a rush basket suspended from his neck, containing a hare and some wild fowl, the produce of his day's sport: he was a tall good looking man, about fifty years of age; was very courteous to his visitors and appeared exceedingly kind and attentive to his wife and family, who evidently regarded him with much respect.

The shops are spacious and plentifully stocked with goods, some of which will suprise the new-comer by their apparent cheapness ; for, instance, he may purchase brandy at seven shillings a gallon, rum at six, and whiskey at two and sixpence ; and the very cheapness of these articles has too often been the means of destruction to the settler. On the opposite bank of the St. Lawrence stands the picturesque village of Point Levi, in which are erected many comfortable villas, and the country around the city is well cultivated by some of the old country farmers, who display the knowledge of a superior system of agriculture.

About ten miles from Quebec, is the interesting village of Indian Lorette, consisting of about one hundred houses, and principally inhabited by Indians of the Huron tribe, with a slight mixture of Canadians. The four chiefs who visited England a few years ago, reside in this place, in very neat and clean wooden houses : they all possess some relics of their visit, hung up in the most conspicuous parts of their dwellings, and appear to set much value on an excellent engraved portrait of his late Majesty George the Fourth. John Vincent, the principal Chief, and who is also styled king of Lorette, has, in addition to the portraits, two medals, one gold, and the other silver, of considerable value, which the king personally presented to him.* There are two extremely neat and clean Catholic churches in the village, one for the Indians' and the other for the Canadians' worship; the former is handsomely decorated with an abundance of images, and the roof bespangled with gilded dots, and is regularly attended by a devout congregation. These Indians, and others of their tribe, receive annual presents from the British Government, as equivalents for their conceded territories.

The passage from Quebec to Montreal is pleasant, particularly in fine weather; the accommoda-

---

* In a visit paid to this village by the author and a party of his friends, the utmost hospitality was exercised towards them; his Majesty was not at home upon their arrival, but the Queen, a good looking Squaw, did the honours and received them very cordially, presenting cakes, maple syrup &c., for their refreshment. Her Majesty with her daughters were busily employed in making fancy baskets for sale, and observed, that she was obliged to work, but that the Queen of England was both paid and kept. In a short time the King returned home, with a rush basket suspended from his neck, containing a hare and some wild fowl, the produce of his day's sport: he was a tall good looking man, about fifty years of age; was very courteous to his visitors and appeared exceedingly kind and attentive to his wife and family, who evidently regarded him with much respect.

In travelling from Quebec to Montreal by land, you continue nearly the whole way on the banks of the river, which is pretty thickly settled by Canadians, not many Europeans being found amongst them.

Montreal is a large, handsome, well-built town, very much improved within these ten years, particularly in the suburbs, which are ornamented by many well-built villas, with gardens attached, in the highest state of culture, and yielding a profusion of fruit and vegetables. Although the distance of Montreal from Quebec is but one hundred and eighty miles, yet so much more forward is the climate of the former, that the vegetables and fruits are at least a month earlier than in the latter place; indeed, the markets of Quebec are regularly supplied from hence with the early summer produce. The orchards in the neighborhood of Montreal are very prolific, and amongst other fruits produce one beautiful apple, called the "pomme-de-gris," of delicious flavor, and vast quantities of which are barrelled, and sent to various parts of the province, and even to France, the country of their first growth, where they are considered as superior to the original fruit.

The Montreal markets are admirably supplied with meat, vegetables, &c., and at a low price;

for instance, beef and mutton, three pence per pound; veal and ham by the quarter, equally low; geese, two shillings and sixpence; turkeys, three to five shillings; fowls, from nine to eighteen pence a couple. In winter, fish, (principally cod and oysters,) are brought hither from the seaport towns in the states, a distance of five or six hundred miles, in a frozen condition; hundreds of pigs, likewise frozen, are transported to the Montreal market. At this season of the year, a general gaiety prevails; an endless throng of sleighs flocking to the town on business or pleasure, their horses caparisoned with jingling bells, and a busy population crowd the streets, intent upon the pursuit of their several avocations. The hotels are the most comfortable places for the sojourn of the traveller, and the charges about a dollar a day, including all expenses—no fees to servants being necessary.

Most of the consignments of goods from England and other parts, to Montreal, are disposed of at public auction; and it is surprising to observe the low prices obtained for the different kinds of manufactured wares, although this may depend in some measure on the supply.

Montreal is justly termed the key to Upper Canada, for here ends the navigation of sea board vessels; consequently, those goods destined for the upper country, are warehoused in the town, and almost all consignments are made to the resident merchants; and although some few of the merchants residing in the upper country, are their own importers, they, for the most part, come to Montreal to make their purchases, which occasions a great interchange of communication with all parts of the upper province.

There are five weekly papers published, each very creditably conducted; the Canadian Courant is of long standing, and has a good circulation; the Montreal Gazette is also ably conducted; the New Montreal Gazette and the Herald belong to one proprietor—the former, a literary publication, generally comprising very interesting matter; the latter with a large advertising patronage, and usually containing much and important information, and the Montreal Herald, which has a more extensive circulation than any. Montreal and its suburbs contain a population of about 50,000, composed of the inhabitants nearly all countries, although by far the greater part are Canadians. The roads near and around the city are excellent, for Mac-Adamizing is now as common here as Day & Martin's blacking; indeed they go hand in hand, for in many parts of the province, where Mac Adams' system has not been adopted, Day & Martin would be an intrusion and a mockery.

Montreal is a busy, bustling town, the shops appear to be well attended with customers, the market filled with various commodities, and the streets thronged with people of all grades. The air in the vicinity of the city is considered more salubrious than in any other part of the Province, which is in consequence of almost all the Signory of Montreal (an Island of about fourteen miles by twenty five) being clear and in a state of cultivation, thus allowing the admission of a thorough current of air to purify the atmosphere; and as a proof of its salubrity, people live to a good old age. Were the forests cleared in the other parts of the Province, and free currents of air admitted, they would be equally healthy, and those local diseases, fever and ague, hardly known.

Many publications have appeared at different times, some containing the most exaggerated statements, which would tend to raise the expectation of the emigrant too highly, and others the grossest errors, and serving only to intimidate him. Should the settler arrive in Canada with agricultural views, let nothing, under any circumstances, or representations, induce him to purchase lands *at home*; he must see and judge for himself. In the first place, the land may not be good, the part of the country may not suit him, there may be no roads, no ways of communication, and many other difficulties only to be ascertained by personal observation.

Canada, in a state of nature, is an universal forest, which is a fact not generally known, and the timber is of little value but for home purposes, and making ashes: it is almost an unerring rule, that the different kinds of timber denote the different qualities of the soil on which they grow; thus, on the best lands will be seen maple, oak, elm, and bass wood and this land will be found best for cultivation; swamps covered with white cedar, (which will make excellent and durable fences,) are converted into the finest meadows; and pine, (either white or red,) beech, birch, or poplar, denote the poorest soil, not altogether unfit for cultivation, but of the worst description. The system of farming here is so different to that pursued in England, that the most inexperienced person, if he be only willing, will soon rival the most skilful agriculturist. Farming implements of every kind are of such different construction, and so easily procured, as to render their importation unnecessary. A person with adequate means would do well to bring a thorough good stud horse, something between the cart and hack, a good young bull, some cows and rams, a mixture of the South Down and Leicester breed. This would be both troublesome and expensive, yet if the imported stock be of good character, it is certain to pay well: it would be of no use to bring inferior cattle, as there are plenty here already, and improvement is only wanted. Furniture, such as bureaus, tables, chairs, or any other heavy kinds of goods, should be purchased here, whilst blankets, bedding, and all kinds of portable goods will prove a valuable investment.

The first step to be taken on arriving, if the land be wild, is to erect a shantee, which is a rough dwelling, composed of logs of wood saddled one on the other at the ends, with a roof, some composed of shingles, some of scoops, that is, halves of the logs of wood, hollowed out, some of slabs, and lastly cvered by the bark of the ash-tree. The chinks are well stuffed with moss, in order to render it warm, the house partitioned off into rooms, and a very comfortable dwelling is erected with little trouble. Persons if they choose, might, even at first, build a frame or a stone house, as stone of the first quality for building is to be had almost every where; but it is more prudent to erect the log hut as above described, and for this reason—when you get a burn on your land, you are very likely, from its running, to burn down the dwelling, and should it be a shantee, the loss will be comparatively nothing.—After the erection, clearing the land must be attended to, commencing to under-brush or cut down all the small trees, not more than six inches in diameter; these should then be collected and piled in heaps. The chopping or cutting down the large trees succeeds, and these are again junked up into lengths of fourteen or fifteen feet each, the tops thrown on the brush heaps. If the land be chopped and underbrushed by contract, the general price is eight dollars an acre; to be chopped, under-brushed, logged-up, burnt, and fenced, sixteen dollars per acre; the best time for underbrushing the land is in the early part of the fall, so that nothing may impede the process of chopping during the winter, for in Canada the ground is covered with snow, generally about eighteen inches deep, from the month of December to the beginning of April: after having chopped the land, it is necessary to wait until the weather becomes dry and warm (which may be expected about the 10th of May,) before the brush-heaps are set on fire, when it will (if properly managed) run regularly through all the land that has been chopped, burning the dry leaves and all the dead vegetable matter accumu-

C

lated on the surface of the soil, and thereby making a good manure. After the burn is completed, the land should be logged up, by putting the junks of the large trees that have been already cut up, into heaps of about twenty together. This should be done by a yoke of oxen and four men. Oxen will be found of the utmost value to a new farmer, being more tractable and steady amongst the stumps and intricate places, than horses, which are apt to plunge and destroy their harness. After the wood is thus piled, it must be burned, and unless either pot or pearl ashes be made, it should be strewn over the ground, as it is an excellent manure.

The choice of the crop depends a great deal on circumstances;—the time when the burn takes place, the nature of the soil, or probably the domestic wants. Should the soil be good, and the logs have happened to be burned about the middle of May—Spring wheat, peas, barley, or oats, may be sown, should either of those kinds of grain be desired; grass seed and clover should be sown with them, as the new settler should always provide himself with pasture land, in order to graze his stock, and cut hay as soon as possible, particularly should he think proper to keep one or more cows. If the soil be rather sandy, and it can be got in order by the 25th of May, Indian corn and pumpkins would be a good crop. The manner of planting the seed is very simple: drop into the ground *four* grains of the corn, removing the mould on either side with a hoe, leaving the distance of a yard between each; and at every fourth, plant a pumpkin-seed, leaving a little hillock about two inches deep on each. Corn thrives infinitely better when planted with pumpkins, for they spread so much over the soil, that they protect the roots of the corn from the rays of the sun, thereby securing to them a degree of moisture. Pumpkins here grow very large, and are, in the fall of the year, an excellent food for pigs; Indian corn is not only a good food for pigs, but it is at all times a marketable article; and is of great service in a family, affording a light and agreeable meal, when made into a kind of thin pudding called *Sepaun*; it is made with little trouble, and eaten with milk or maple molasses. Indian meal is also an excellent substitute for wheat flour, and is made into cakes called johnny cakes; when mixed with a portion of flour, it makes a bread, that for delicacy or lightness is not be surpassed. In the winter of 1829, the wheat crop having partially failed, many people substituted the johnny cakes for bread throughout the winter.

Potatoes will do well in a sandy soil, and are more valuable than any other crop to the new farmer, as they will serve both himself and his cattle : the very finest potatoes are raised here, particularly when they grow in a new soil, not being so good where the land has been a few years under cultivation. The returns of the crops that are to be expected, vary according to the soil and manner of its tillage, but the following is the general average. First, spring-wheat seldom gives more than twenty bushels to the acre, winter-wheat from thirty to fifty, barley, in good land about forty, oats thirty to forty, peas about twenty five ; Indian corn is the most prolific and gives a return of upwards of four hundred per cent, but being thinly planted it seldom returns more than from thirty to thirty five bushels to the acre : it thrives best in a dry season ; forming in its first growth a kind of funnel which retains the moisture of the dew (which is here very heavy) nearly the whole day : it vegetates rapidly, having been known to spring six inches in twenty four hours, and grows to the height of nine or ten feet, and when at its growth, and in bloom, it presents a very beautiful appearance. Mr. Cobbett has informed us, that all the Indian corn he has grown in England, has been of the dwarf kind ; and it always will be so :

for the climate is not congenial to its production. Potatoes, independently of their excellent quality, give a very large return, from two hundred and fifty to three hundred and fifty bushels the acre.

To emigrants of some property, the oldest settled parts of the country will generally be found the most desirable: the settlements on the St. Lawrence, near and above Brockville to Kingston, thence to York, and far above it, the roads will be found excellent, and the society, for the most part, respectable. Good mechanics would find ample encouragement in most of the towns, and smiths and carpenters would do well in the country settlements. Professional men have generally the ability to judge for themselves in the choice of situation, but it may be observed that there is a large field for the exercise of their respective talents. As regards the law, that in operation in the upper provinces is founded upon the rules of English practice, which however unequal in some respects, however capable of being converted into an engine of oppression in the hand of unprincipled practitioners, is yet superior to the code of the lower province, and in the hands of men of honor and integrity may work for the general good. In Upper Canada the transfer of property is duly protected, and its investment whether it be personal or real, secured according to the wishes of the owner. In Lower Canada, on the contrary, under the operation of the French law, a man may buy an estate, commence improvements, and occupy his soil in the expectation that he has secured a home for life, when at the expiration of three or four years, in comes a mortgagee, and wrests his property from him; there is scarcely a possibility of guarding against this misfortune, as no law exists for the registry of conveyances or mortgages. Again, a wife on her death bed can, by virtue of the same, law, absolutely will and make over one half of the property to her children or even to strangers, to the total exclusion of her husband. These are evils that loudly call for redress.

There is also room in the Upper Province for medical men, and particularly for those who can reconcile themselves to live in the country, and unite a little agricultural with medical practice. There is no lack of employment, although it too frequently happens that in the event of an accident, the patient has to be brought to the doctor, some twenty or thirty miles, instead of the doctor visiting the patient, and for a very simple reason: in addition to the medical charge, the practitioner requires (and properly so,) so much for his travelling expences, for without this regulation he could not possibly attend upon distant cases, in a country where travelling is so tedious and so frequently delayed : it therefore happens, that as the poor man cannot pay for the journey of his doctor, in addition to his attendance, he must neccessarily seek his abode for treatment.

The poor, but healthy emigrant, desirous of employment can readily obtain it either in the neighbourhood of the public works, or in the distant districts of the Province ; if he possess a small sum and be anxious to settle on land, his wishes may easily be gratified, when his own prudence and industry will afford him the present means of support, and the future prospect of independence ; let him refrain from the vice of intemperance, take plenty of exercise in the open air, retire with the sun, and again rise with him, and he will experience the full enjoyment of health, and improve both his moral and bodily strength. The appetite created by exercise and labour, will be satisfied with simple aliment, and the excellent pork, that he can raise himself or purchase at a very cheap rate will suffice for his general diet. An absurd remark was made in one of the papers in the last fall, that the common food, fried pork and potatoes, was injurious to the health of the emigrants ; to this it may be replied that the abuse of spirituous liquors causes two thirds of the sickness in these provinces, that the food complained of is sufficiently good and nourishing, and that it has never been and can never be productive of any evil to the laboring classes of the community. As the means of the settler increase, his additional comforts are provided for; his fall cattle supply him not only with a variety of food, but with the materials for the manufacture of his soap and candles; his wants are nearly all supplied by his farm, and he commences his independent existence through the continued exercise of his industry.

There is always a great variety of lands both in a wild and cultivated state for sale by private individuals, the description of which may be found in the different newspapers.

The Canada Company may be regarded as the principal body, through whom lands are obtained; their chief office is in York, but in almost every town they have established an agent, and books of reference are left in many respectable taverns for the information of the public. The company have had a large tract of land surveyed on the borders of Lake Huron; it lies about one hundred and eighty miles north west of York, and though there are many places even farther distant that are desirable for occupation, having excellent roads and a continuation of good settlements, yet the Huron tract is as yet much too far in the wilderness, and is but thinly peopled. The company have lands for sale in all the upper Provinces, but as ample opportunities offer themselves in the more settled parts, there is no necessity of going so far into the wilderness. Large portions of those extensive tracts of land granted by government to military officers and others for past services, remain in their original forest state, without cultivation of any kind, and with their townships less improved than any others in the Province. The reason of this may be traced to the impolicy of giving three or four lots to one man who is thus in all probability unable to improve his land in the same ratio as those around him; there are unquestionably many characters who from former services, are fully entitled to the reward they have received in such grants, but since it is the aim of this new country to cement the interests of society by thickly and well settled townships, and thereby ensure the erection of churches, schools, and mills, as well as the formation of good roads, the *claims* should be equalized as much as possible, in order to render the contribution of labour to the general service of equal value to each individual, in the advantages secured. It must be admitted, that the military townships are the least improved of any in the province; large blanks of uncultivated land are sometimes observed, and in their original forest clothing, while all around them is fertility. This disposition of the land leads to another inconvenience in preventing the church from being built in the centre of the township; or where the greater part of the inhabitants are settled, and as the roads in such situations are generally very bad, a large portion of the population are debarred the ability of attending divine service, as well from the distance from the church, as from the difficulty of reaching it on account of the roads.

The price of wild land averages from one to four dollars an acre through the Province, but in the immediate vicinity of towns, from six to eight; the usual terms are, that one fourth of the purchase money be paid down, and the remainder by equal yearly instalments. Should the emigrant purchase his lands either of Government or the Company, the title is unquestionable, but when he deals with private individuals, he should employ at once, a respectable attorney, as there is a mode sometimes practised in order to dupe the unwary; the settler buys a block of ground, and pays the first instalment, the vendor then, instead of returning the deed, gives a bond promising to produce the deed at some future day, when probably the land is not absolutely his own property; he disappears and the purchaser has no redress The deed for the land should always be executed on the first instalment being paid, and lodged in the hands of some respectable third party for the due protec- of all, for even where no chicanery is intended, the original possessor might die before the deed is due, and it would be very difficult to find his h eirs, executors, &c. A person, with ready cash might purchase a very good farm of two hundred acres, with from fifty to seventy acres under cultivation, well fenced, with a dwelling-house, barn &c., for about three hundred pounds, which is the most prudent beginning in a new country for those who have the means.

The price of good Canadian horses is about £25 the pair, or span, as they are called: these are a kind of small cart horse, well adapted for this country. Cows fetch from four to six pounds; oxen from fifty to eighty-five dollars the pair or yoke: sheep from two to four dollars each: young pigs taken from the sow at a month, one dollar, two months old, seven shillings and six pence; good store pigs from three to five dollars. A barrel of salt pork, containing two hundred pounds of meat, from twelve to twenty two dollars;

a barrel of flour containing one hundred and ninety six pounds, from six to nine dollars. Wheat was sold in Montreal during the last season for six shillings, and six and nine pence a bushel ; at York five shillings and seven pence half penny (or as it is termed nine N. Y. shillings) has been the current price throughout the season; above York, at Dundas, Hamilton, and their neighbourhoods, the price has been five shillings. When a Canadian farmer can procure a dollar a bushel for his wheat, he has no right to complain. Oats at Montreal will bring at an average price, one shilling and six pence a bushel ; at Kingston the same ; and at York from fifteen to eighteen pence ; peas about three shillings ; barley three shillings and four pence, and more of this grain is required than is at present grown in the upper province : potatoes generally average about one shilling and six pence a bushel.

On the Ottawa river, where the timber trade is carried on, to its largest extent, oats and hay fetch a much better price than elsewhere, but in the other products there is little or no difference. In the last winter the Ottawa oats realized two shillings and in the spring they commanded a ready sale at three shillings and six pence a bushel : hay while selling at Kingston, York, and some other places for ten dollars a ton, brought from twelve to fifteen on the Ottawa.

The general price of Indian corn over the Provinces, is from two and nine pence to three shillings and three pence a bushel. A good sized fat ox will bring from eight to ten pounds, and a young ox for work is of the same value from their constant employment as beasts of draught; indeed, an ox is not fattened for the butcher until it is growing old. Butter and cheese made in Canada find a ready and profitable sale.

It is necessary to observe that the prices here named refer to the Halifax currency, as it is termed; there is a considerable difference in the value of Canadian and English money, amounting at the usual rate of exchange to about seventeen per cent. The English shilling passes for fourteen pence; the dollar, worth in the British Isles about four shillings and two pence, is circulated as five shillings; the English sovereign is worth one pound, three shillings and four pence; so that an emigrant bringing out one hundred sovereigns, is nominally worth one hundred and sixteen pounds, fourteen shillings and four pence. It is a subject of some importance to the traveller to be able to calculate his expences, particularly in this, his newly adopted country. If he ascend the St. Lawrence in the direction of York or Kingston, or any intermediate place, the fare may be secured on to

Prescott, which in the cheapest manner of travelling will cost about three dollars a head. The steam navigation does not extend lower down than Prescott. When at this place, if the settler intend to proceed up the country, he may embark on board the steamer to Kingston, in the best cabin for five dollars, in the steerage for one dollar; to York for ten dollars in the cabin, in the steerage for two. There are no perquisites required either in packet and stage travelling or in the taverns, indeed a servant would regard the offer of a gratuity in the light of an insult. There are now three large steam boats running from Prescott to York, the Niagara, the Queenston and the Alciope; a very large boat upon nearly double the scale of any of them is now building by the Messrs. Hamiltons of Prescott, which will be afloat this summer, and of course render the facilities in travelling, even greater than they are at present. If it be the object of the settler to locate himself on the Ottawa, at By-town, or in its neighbourhood, he may proceed from Lachine about ten miles from Montreal to Point Fortune, for three dollars, from thence to Hawksbury by land for five shillings, and from Hawksbury to By-town, a distance of sixty miles, for another three dollars. In this route, the pleasing evidence of agricultural improvement will be recognized between Montreal and Lachine, whilst well finished and regular built houses, neat and thriving farms, and an endless and fanciful variety of gardens greet the eye in every direction. Lachine is a long straggling village on the water side, with nothing particular to invite the attention of the voyager; from this place the journey may be continued through lake St. Louis, and about fourteen miles above Lachine, the junction of the noble rivers, the St. Lawrence, and the Ottawa, may be observed running their course side by side through the lake, without an admixture of their waters. A dark reddish stream marks the track of the Ottawa, while that of the St. Lawrence is distinguished by its clear blue colour; the separate courses of the rivers are thus continued, until the rapids of Carillon are gained, when the violence of the current unites them in one impetuous flow. The military post of Coteau de lac where Government retains a small garrison, next receives the traveller, from whence sometimes by batteaux, (large boats) and sometimes by land, an easy passage is secured to Prescott. This is a comfortable little town, with many good houses and stores, and the country around is well cultivated. Prescott is rendered of some importance from its situation, as being the place where the regular navigation terminates, and the opposite town to Ogdensburg on the American side of the St. Lawrence, and which is a place of considerable size and importance. The communication between the two places is almost hourly, by means of tow boats, which have to cross a channel about a mile in breadth. The traveller here, has a ready opportunity of visiting our enterprising neighbours, but he may be reminded that no contraband trade can be carried on, as the authorities on each side are sufficiently attentive in the performance of their respective duties. In the summer time, the life and gaiety of Prescott are greatly increased by the numerous arrivals to and departures from the upper parts of the Province. It is desirable that individuals, as they are passing through the country (unless they are bound to some particular spot) should look at the newspapers in the various places through which they pass, as farms and situations for location are frequently advertised, on the line of route, some of which may correspond with their means and inclinations. These inquiries may occasionally be productive of a little delay, but the time thus occupied, so far from being lost, will both lend useful information, and probably supply to the inquirer a comfortable home.

As the St. Lawrence is still ascended, the scenery on the north bank is well deserving attention; thus, the British side is agreeably diversified with good stone residences, large orchards and gardens well stocked with fruit trees of every description, and many neat and even handsome little villages. This part of the country is chiefly remarkable for the large quantities of pot and pearlashes manufactured. An emigrant who purchases a lot of wild land, on which there is abundance of elm, ash, maple, and bass-wood timber, may, if the price of the articles be tolerably good in Montreal, (say from 30 to £35 a ton for pot, and from 33 to £38 for pearl ashes) pay the expenses of clearing the land, provided he chooses to risk the first outlay. The expense of erecting a pot ashery is not heavy, and the process of manufacture is very simple. The whole outlay if but one kettle be employed, is from 30 to £35; if the kettles be used, it may amount to fifty pounds. Having the leeches erected (that is, large tubs with holes in the bottoms) its flooring is strewed with lime about eight inches thick, trod down hard; the leech is then filled with ashes, and watered regularly until their strength is completely extracted; during the time the leeches are running, the ley already procured from them is kept boiling for about two days and a night, when it forms a consistency called "black salts." If pearl ash be the object, these salts are taken out of the kettle, and placed in an oven erected for the purpose, and there by a process of evaporation, formed into the desired material. Should the intention be merely to make a pot ash, the boiling is continued until all the ley is procured that from eighty to one hundred bushels of ashes will supply: as the water evaporates, the mass assumes a variety of different colours, such as green, blue, yellow, &c., and at length an extreme fire being kept up, it presents a consistent surface of the colour of melted lead, which is then drawn off or ladled out into iron pans to cool, forming in this last process, the substance denominated potash. Pot and pearl ashes are two of the principle staples of Canada, and are of essential importance, both as an export and for domestic use, and so well is their value understood, as to induce the preservative of all the ashes produced by the fires of the family, which are readily disposed of to the potash manufacturers in the neighbourhood.

About twelve miles above Prescott, stands the handsome town of Brockville, so named from the late distinguished General Sir Isaac Brock; it has been built since the last American war, and now contains upwards of three thousand inhabitants.

The river begins to widen at this place, or in other words, to put on the appearance of a lake; and about twenty miles above Brockville, Lake Ontario itself is perceived. The river scenery is now greatly enlivened by the steam-boats and timber rafts, especially in the spring of the year; on these rafts, little cabins made of the bark of trees are erected, presenting the appearance at a distance of many immense bee-hives, and by this conveyance, merchandize, yokes of oxen, and the commodities permitted to be brought to Canada from the American side, are readily transported.

Amongst the variety of American produce thus received into Canada, the most singular consists of whole cargoes of pigs, brought on the rafts, two or three hundred at a time. Live stock pay a very low duty, and hence our neighbours find these pigs a very profitable article of commerce.

Lake Ontario now commences, and the first place in this route on its borders, is Kingston, a large and well built town, and the principal naval station on the Lake. Its appearance has been considered somewhat like that of Portsmouth, in England, and the resemblance is assisted by its white cliffs, and by some large ships that are here laid up in ordinary. The St. Lawrence, a line of battle-ship pierced for 130 guns, two frigates, some

D

sloops, &c., attach a character to this safe and excellent harbour. Kingston is altogether (if the expression be orthodox) a fresh-water sea-port town; is clean, large, and well built, and may already be ranked as a place of great importance. The markets are exceedingly well supplied from the cultivated lands in the neighbourhood; and it is the residence of a great number of opulent and highly respectable inhabitants. It has of late years been supposed by some individuals, that the seat of government would be removed from York to Kingston; but the building a new house of assembly at York, together with other preparations, contradict the assumption that the legislatorial offices will be removed. As a commercial town, Kingston ranks the second in Upper Canada, although her prosperity received a serious blow, a few years since, from the effects of which she is but just recovering. The consequences of free trade were bitterly experienced in Canada, and Kingston in particular suffered. A want of confidence prevailed, the colonial bank paper was depreciated, and at length the bank compelled to suspend its payments, and wind up its accounts. These circumstances are now happily contrasted by the prevailing prosperity; a second bank has been established in the town through the exertions of Christopher Hagerman, the representative for Kingston, and Solicitor General of Upper Canada, who introduced and carried through the House of Assembly a bill for its incorporation. The establishment of banks in any part of the country always is positive and pleasing evidence of prosperity; and as they lend means to industry and enterprize in prosecuting undertakings for public as well as individual advantage, they must be considered as contributing towards the real interests of the country at large.

Kingston will probably become a place of much importance, as well from its central situation in the province, as for being the principal naval station. In the neighbourhood, the population is greatly increasing, and thriving townships appear in quick succession on that land, which a few years ago presented the desolation of the wilderness, and had scarcely been passed by the foot of man. The bear and the wolf held undisputed range, where the fertile meadow and the farm yard now exist: these marauders are still more plentiful than desirable, but they recede in proportion to the advance of settlers, and in a few years the country may be freed from them altogether.

Should the route from Montreal to Upper Canada be preferred by way of Ottawa, and through the heart of the country from By-town to Kingston, the journey may be made either by land or water from Montreal to Point Fortune: in the journey by land, the traveller continues in lower Canada until he reaches Grenville, (40 miles) which is opposite to Point Fortune; on the road are many Canadian villages, although in this part of the lower Province there are more British settlers than elsewhere, St. Anne's is a pretty rural village on the banks of the Ottawa, and it was here that the Irish bard, Thomas Moore, composed his "Canadian Boat Song." At Grenville, the Government are making a canal, twelve miles in length, in order to avoid the rapids of the Long Sault: for some time the work was not carried on with the energy and expedition which marked the progress of the Rideau canal, although it is now continued with greater rapidity; and when finished it will be of the utmost consequence to the navigation of the Ottawa. The voyage from Grenville to By-town is performed in a steamboat in rather less than 12 hours, whereas four years ago it employed 30 hours; at that time there was scarcely a settler between the two places, but now on both banks of the river there is an astonishing change; although on the Lower Canada side of the Ottawa, with the exception of its immediate banks, the country is wholly in a state of nature. For many hundreds or even thousands of miles, this part of Canada has never been thoroughly explored; a small party went in this direction about two years since, but they returned with no other information than that there were some lakes and beaver meadows, in that section of the Province; and as it doubtless contains much fertile land, it is to be lamented that it has not been properly explored. On the approach to By-town, the scenery which bursts most unexpectedly on the view, is scarcely to be surpassed for its boldness and sublimity: the first objects that strike the attention are the Rideau falls about two miles below the town; these are two distinct falls, which rush over the precipice in the form of a curtain from a height of about fifty feet: the Union Bridge (so called from connecting the upper and lower Province by crossing the Ottawa, which is the boundary line between them) now opens to the view, and presents a piece of architecture that reflects the highest credit on those who accomplished such a gigantic undertaking; the current of the river is here broken by tremendous rocks, on which rest the abutments of the bridge; the centre arch forms a span of two hundred and seventy feet, which may give some idea of the immense labour and difficulty required in its accomplishment : it is let at a yearly rent of about £200, each foot passenger paying a penny, horses two pence, and so on.

Immediately above the bridge are the falls extending across the Ottawa, called the " Chandiere Falls," these assume all imaginable forms, but it is in the winter, when the river is frozen over, that they present the most interesting appearance : the ice accumulates to the very edge of the falls, and in congealed masses down the ledges of the rocks, becoming transparently white from the intense freezing, and forming apertures through which the dark red waters of the Ottawa rush with an inconceivable fury, the foam casting up the frozen particles, which, from the rays of the sun, assume every variety of hue. The Union Bridge leads from Bytown to the village of Hull ; which is now a very large and well settled township ; it owes its first settlement to Mr. Philemon Wright, who came to this spot about thirty years ago, when not a tree was cut.

Mr. Wright, justly called the father of the township, is an American gentleman, who has given proofs of an enterprising and persevering mind ; he has lived to see his numerous followers arrive at a state of comparative affluence, and as the country in which the township is situated is entitled, from its increased population, to send a member to the house of Assembly, Mr. Wright has, very properly, been returned this last election as its representative, and since that period an additional member has been elected. The township of Hull is skirted by a ridge of mountains, being a continuation of that chain, which is seen for some distance at the back of Quebec; they are supposed to extend for some thousands of miles, and are even believed to be a continuation of the Andes in South America. A part of the mountains near Hull have been explored and are found to contain, deeply embedded, great quantities of iron and lead ore, black lead and marble, and some minerals, and although it is probable that coals might be found, none have been yet discovered; the iron ore produces 75 per cent. or three fourths of iron. These mines have not hitherto been worked, from the want of persons competent to the undertaking, both as respects pecuniary means, and ability to engage in the task. But a field of enterprize is doubtless open to the individual who would commence a search for the treasures contained in the bowels of the earth; at present a vast mass of property lies dormant and utterly useless, but let it be redeemed, and immediate opportunity is offered of transporting it to a scene of usefulness, as By-town is not more than 12 miles distant, and there are various other places that would participate in the advantage, and reward a spirited projector.

By-town, independently of its close connection with the Rideau canal, will in all probability become a large and important place; both from its central situation in a fertile and well settled country, from its close connection with the lumber trade of the Ottawa, and from its importance as a place of strength and safety in the event of a war; all combine to warrant the supposition that By-town may ere long become a place of considerable importance; but the furtherance of its prosperity will be very much retarded if the means available be not at hand; many men who have ability and energy for large undertakings and who have also a bona fide property though not available, cannot procure discounts at either bank in the Province; the distance is too far, the parties are not known—thus rendering it impossible although a part of the country is in a healthy state of commerce and growing prosperity, and there are objects of enterprize which, with the assistance of available capital would be productive of the best consequences to its immediate neighborhood, in the diffusion of wealth to the surrounding country, and hence of conferring immense benefit to the Province generally.

The state both of trade and agriculture in the vicinity of the Ottawa, is very prosperous; therefore their united financial wants call for the establishment of a bank in By-town. We have before enlarged on the importance of such an institution in other parts of this new country, and regarded it as the means, from whence an encouragement to industry might be derived; the same result would succeed were a similar assistance in the shape of a bank, granted to the several interests of this populous and flourishing neighbourhood. The arguments against banks are founded upon contracted notions of public policy, and the absurd desire of rendering three fourths of a whole population dependent upon the remaining fourth, for the necessary degree of support and assistance.

When a country generally is in a state unable to bear its burthens, when commerce is forced beyond its proper limits, a circulating paper only acts with advantage as a prop to a decayed building, which the longer it is kept up, the more sudden will be the crash of the structure; but in a young and rising country whose sources of wealth are but just in the bud, when the legitimate objects of commerce are only just beginning to develop themselves, but yet possess an absolute though unavailable property, here local banks are indispensable; they are the very veins through which the wealth of a country flows to its natural and proper channel.

The township of Hull, Mr. Wright's settlement, is mostly settled by American natives, a very respectable body of people who give substantial proofs of unwearied industry and application. Hull is a remarkable thriving and well settled township; in which several very substantial lumber merchants reside; but there are two brothers, in partnership, remarkable for the extensive business they carry on in this trade. Their christian names are Job and David, and by which they seem to be equally well known from Quebec to the pine regions; these individuals are entirely indebted to their industry and perseverance for the advantages they possess, and which are conspicuous in the surrounding neighbourhood; if a traveller in this neighbourhood demand to whom such and such a raft of timber belongs, the answer will frequently be, 'Job and David;' if a handsome span of horses are on the road, the same reply may be given to a similar question, and so of other species of property of which these reputable individuals claim the ownership. The partners reside together in a long white house on the Hull road, about two miles from the Union Bridge.

The inhabitants of this part of the country are well disposed towards one another, and readily contribute their assistance in cases of urgency; when a settler is unable to hire laborers, and yet wishes to erect a house, build up a barn, log up his land &c., he calls a bee, as it is termed, and which simply consists in summoning all his neighbors to his assistance; this plan of mutual aid also prevails amongst the females, who raise bees for sewing, knitting, making up bedding, or for any other domestic purpose; thus through a general spirit of kindness, very considerable undertakings are accomplished, which would have been beyond the reach of individual effort. There is a trait in the character of this population, that deserves honorable mention; that is, strict honesty, of which one pleasing instance may be offered: Captain S. a highly respectable gentleman, who had returned from the naval service, and is now a resident on the opposite side of the Ottawa, when he first contemplated a settlement in the country, visited the Upper Canada side of the river, then a complete wilderness; during the period of three or four months, he left his goods on the Hull side of the river to the amount of seven or eight hundred pounds, including many articles of a portable nature, in a mere shed with scarcely any fastening, and although this was by the river side, he found upon the removal of his property, that he had not lost the slightest article.

There are new settlements forming in all the intermediate places on the Lower Canada side between Hull and the Chats, about thirty miles distant; and which is becoming a place of considerable importance. Here are the falls of the Chats, consisting of fifteen distinct falls, extending to a distance of two miles across the Ottawa; and between each fall there is a clump of pine trees; these falls are extremely novel from their regularity; and here nature seems to have copied art, for almost all the fifteen except the centre fall are nearly uniform; the centre is precisely in the shape of a horse shoe, and it still adds to the interest of this scene that at a distance of about twenty feet from the bottom of the centre fall, the water in a circumference of perhaps twenty or thirty feet, bubbles or boils up to a height of ten or twelve feet above the surface of the river, and has the perfect appearance of a foaming cauldron. A gentleman, Mr. White, one of the principal contractors of the Rideau canal, has lately made a purchase of some property adjoining, and is about to carry on considerable improvements. He is now preparing to build a steam-boat, to run from the Chats to Bytown, when in operation, which will give a new life to this part of the country. The Hudson Bay Company have their first boat established at the Chats, and the Company of late years having lost so many ships in the passage round by sea, intend, it is said, in future, to make the Ottawa their regular route to their principal forts and posts in Hudson's Bay. Above the Chats are some new settlements, Clarenden and Mac Nab. This latter settlement was established by a Scottish chief of that name. " Laird Mac Nab" of Mac Nab, who has prevailed on a great many settlers to join him from Scotland, and the system he adopts in his little colony is somewhat similar to the old Scottish customs.

The country above the Chats is not much settled; indeed at the distance of thirty or forty miles the pine regions commence, where the red or Norway timber trees are the sole possessors of the soil. These groves are supposed to extend for hundreds of miles, although the country in their direction has only been partially explored. In the fall of each year, a considerable number of persons visit this tract of country, remaining until the following spring, to prepare the timber for market.

Near the Chats is the township of Fitzroy but partially settled, and adjoining it is Ramsay a respectable and populous township; nearer By-town are Goulburn and Huntley, both thickly settled, the latter containing some of the best lands in the Province. On the front of the Ottawa, are Tarbolton and March, both thinly settled, although containing many respectable officers who have retired from public service.

The whole of this part of the province being colder than the western portion, is perhaps not so well adapted to the pursuits of agriculture; but it still presents many advantages to the settler, the chief of which may be considered the healthiness of its climate.

The river Ottawa abounds with fish, supplying to the settlers on its margin a vast supply of delicious and wholesome food; in the summer season pleasure can be joined with business in their capture as they come down the small streams in shoals; when dried and salted they make a good store food for the winter. The largest fish in the Ottawa is the Masquinonger, averaging from twenty to forty pounds weight, and resembling the pike in colour and in the shape of the head, but infinitely superior in flavor. The cat-fish, so called from its near resemblance to that animal, may be considered the most valuable fish of the Ottawa; they are sufficiently fat not to require any butter or pork in cooking, and are regarded, with justice, as an excellent and nourishing food. In addition to these are the pike, the perch, sun-fish (a small flat fish having the appearance of a sun on the side) the bass, the white fish, succer mullet, eel, pickerel, &c. They are easily caught, and will take almost any bait that is given them, either a bit of pork, frog, or should nothing else offer, a piece of an old moccasin.

The Ottawa also produces the sword fish, very formidable either in or out of the water; it is destructive to the other species of fish, and when caught will be found most troublesome to disengage from the hook, as it snaps in a most formidable manner with its double row of sharp teeth.

Not half a century ago, the banks of the Ottawa were peopled almost entirely by Indians of the different hunting tribes, Micmacs, Shawnees, &c.; they have now wholly retired from these parts, and are not to be found in any numbers within two or three hundred miles above the Chats, occasionally coming down to dispose of their furs. They have, for the most part no settled habitation, but live a roaming life, with all their little wealth, (consisting generally of a few blankets, a gun, some traps, iron pots, and a few other necessaries,) in their canoes.

They are, when unmolested, a harmless, inoffensive race; but in their wars amongst themselves, they practise the most barbarous cruelties. If once offended, they are implacable, and never forgive an injury. When the North West Company existed, one of the gentlemen connected with that Company, had by some means offended an Indian with whom they dealt in furs; this gentleman had occasion to go to England immediately, and did not return for five years. When he did return, it was soon known to the Indian, who was seen one morning lurking about the fort with a loaded gun. He was taken into the fort and asked his purpose; he candidly owned that he waited the appearance of such a gentleman, whom he meant to shoot. For his treachery he was hanged without ceremony.

Their entire occupation, during the winter months, is hunting wild animals, such as the beaver, martin, mink, otter, &c., for their furs. The beaver, the most valuable on account of its fur, is getting somewhat scarce. The Hudson Bay Company have therefore adopted the plan of preventing their hunting Indians from catching them in traps as formerly, lest they should kill the young as well as the old, and thus destroy the race.

The beavers are the most sagacious of the animal creation: they clear meadows, make dams, and excavate their little canals; fell trees, build their houses; and all with the utmost order and regularity. When they fell a tree, they gnaw it away on one side, so that it shall fall exactly in the position they wish: their water-dams are made in the shape of a horse-shoe, and arranged as regularly as though it were done by the hand of man. They live in communities of from twenty to thirty, and should one happen to be lazy, they beat him unmercifully, and will not suffer him to remain among them. These discarded beavers are often met with by the hunters, and are always in a lean condition. They live principally on the inner part of the white birch, which they store up in large quantities in the summer for their winter food. These animals work early in the morning and in the evening. The manner of erecting their winter habitations is very curious;—one of the large beavers will lie on its back, whilst several of the others load it with mud; of which, by holding its legs in a particular position, it contrives to hold a large quantity; and when fully laden, the other beavers take hold of its tail with their teeth, and draw it to the spot fixed on for their winter abode. This is several times repeated, the carrier coming regularly back with the rest. They build the house on piles at the curve of the dam, with a floor raised above the water to keep them dry : it is about six feet in diameter and quite round, with a hole at the bottom to enable them to make their escape in case of alarm. A regular roof is formed of twigs well cemented with mud. These animals possess amazing strength in their tails, with which they collect the mud for their building, plaster the sides of the house, drive the piles to support the dam to a considerable depth in the ground, and use it wherever the force of a hammer is required ; they are very broad and long.

The Indians of the Ottawa appear to have little or no idea of cultivation ; some few grow a little Indian corn, but they mostly depend on chance for their subsistence. In the summer they make canoes, and bring their furs down the river; these bark canoes of the most exact shape, that will contain twenty men besides a ton e and a half of loading with the greatest safety, are simply made and the only tool they make use of is a pocket knife, not even a nail being required in their formation.

They are passionately fond of spirits, and the worst results often occur from their intoxication; for when in this state the greatest impositions are frequently practised on them. Their mode of trading away their skins is singular; should they have a hundred or more skins, they will only sell one at a time; and when sober, they are very acute, and take good care to get their value; but when intoxicated, they part with them for little or nothing,—frequently a good beaver skin for a small glass of rum: and many a designing person, well aware of this propensity, encourage it in order to defraud them, and have made much money by these nefarious practises.

Some of the squaws when young, are interesting, good looking girls, and were they not to distort their features in the manner they do, by slitting the gristle of their nose, &c., they really might be termed handsome. The cruelties these Indians practice on the prisoners whom they capture in their wars, are enormities of the most revolting nature, viz: scalping, taking out their eyes, cutting out their tongues, and in this state making them walk over the burning embers of large fires, uttering on those occasions the most horrid yells and groans.

The Micmacs and Shawnees had been at war for a long time. It is their practice in warfare for the

Indians to go about in parties of from twenty to thirty. On one of these occasions a band of the Shawnees headed by a son of their chief named Winneewee, attacked a camp of the Micmacs under their chief (Caunawana); the chief himself escaped, but the Shawnees took some of his tribe and some squaws; amongst them the only daughter of Caunawana the chief of the Micmacs. She was an interesting young creature about seventeen, and for a squaw, handsome. The Shawnees had to take their prisoners some three or four days march to their camp, for the subordinate Indians are not allowed to perform the office of scalping &c., till the prisoners are brought before their chief, who generally performs this horrible rite himself. In marching them to the camp of Winneewee, his son the young chief became violently attached to the daughter of Caunawana, their female captive. And when they arrived at his father's camp, the young chief most earnestly implored her rescue. Winneewee became outrageous at the thoughts of his son forming on attachment to the daughter of his implacable enemy, and threatened the young chief with instant death if he persisted. His passion was however too deeply rooted to allow even the wrath of his father to remove it,—and he still continued to implore his consent, so that at last he told his son, that if he would bring him seven heads of the Micmacs before the setting of seven suns, he would give him up the daughter of Caunawana. The young chief was not long in prevailing on a band of stout young Indians to join him in his undertaking, and within the given time, he brought to his father the required ransom, and obtained the object of his wishes.

About two years afterwards, a strong party of the Micmacs surprised and carried a camp of the Shawnees taking several prisoners together with the son of Winneewee, badly wounded, and the young squaw his wife. The Micmacs took their prisoners to the camp of Caunawana to undergo the usual cruelties and death. The young squaw well knew the violence of her father, and that if she attempted to intercede either for herself or the young chief her husband, that a more horrible death awaited them both. They therefore made up their minds to their fate.

The Micmacs have a peculiar custom of marking their children of both sexes when young, by slitting the gristle of their noses. When arrived at the camp of Caunawana, the young squaw was the first brought forth to undergo the horrible ordeal. Before the first operation is begun of peeling the scalp off the head, a tight bandage is bound round their eyes.

Caunawana, stepping forward to make the first dreadful gash, stayed his knife for he saw it was a Micmac ; and on examining her more closely, he beheld in the person of his intended victim, his own and only daughter. The savage breast was not unsusceptible of kindred feeling. His daughter, now aware of his discovery, implored in the most supplicating manner that he would not stay the operation, unless in restoring her he also released her husband, the young chief. Caunawana overjoyed at again seeing his daughter, whom he had long given up for dead, released her husband with all the other prisoners, which was the means of restoring peace between these two warlike tribes.

Wolves here, as well as elsewhere, are most destructive animals. They roam in the forest, and when driven by hunger, sometimes come into the clearances and commit dreadful havoc amongst the cattle. They hunt in packs, frequently catch deer, and when they get one, every atom of the skin and flesh is devoured in a few hours. Their ravages amongst cattle may be avoided with care and precaution. There is a premium paid for their destruction ; five dollars in the Upper and ten in the Lower Province, yet they are more numerous in Upper Canada. This distinction of premium is bad policy, and well worth the attention of the

House of Assembly, for it is by no means the least evil that a settler has to contend with.

The object of the premium is of course to rid the country of those destructive animals, and the wording of the act made for this purpose is "that if the parties take the heads and skins to a magistrate and make oath, that he or they killed the wolf or wolves in the province, they shall, by presenting his certificate to the treasurer of the respective district, be paid the allowed premium."

It happened a short time ago, that a settler who resided in the Upper Province, (where, as was before observed, the premium is only five dollars each,) trapped a she wolf, which was at the time big with young. A neighbor, an American, having heard of the circumstance, went to the settler and purchased the live wolf. He fed her well, and in a little time she brought forth a litter of eight young ones. He immediately got a cage made, and took the whole family of live wolves into the nearest part of the Lower Province, there killed them, and received the premium of ten dollars for each.

The black bears are numerous here. In their native state they are a very different looking animal than when in confinement. In the summer, when fat, they have rather a noble looking appearance; in the winter they are never to be met with. They take to

E3

54 CANADA AS IT IS.

their dens, large holes in the rocks, or earth, and remain in them till the beginning of May. They lay up no stores whatever for their winter supplies, but exist in a state of somnolence. When they return to their dens they are fat and sleek, but when they first make their appearance in the spring, they are mere skeletons. In the summer they subsist on roots, wild fruits, Indian corn, and in fact every thing that comes in their way; they sometimes do a great deal of mischief amongst the grain, not alone from the quantity they consume, but they roll about and beat down the standing grain, thus destroying it. They are frequently killed in committing these depredations, but their smell is so keen that it requires caution to get near them. The general plan is to erect a stage about twelve feet high, so that their approach may be observed. They are frequently also caught in traps.

The black is the only species of bear in Canada; but towards the North Western Territory there are three other kinds, the white, the brown, and the yellow. The white bear is one of the fiercest animals in existence. They never show mercy to any living creature, not even to their own species amongst the male kind, for whenever they meet, one if not both is sure to die, and hence their scarcity. The yellow bear is also very scarce; the coat of the yellow bear is supposed to be the finest hair in the world.

Canada produces three kinds of deer,—the red, which is the most common, the fallow, and the moose deer; the last is a most extraordinary animal, and not frequently met with;—it is of such an enormous height, that a horse of sixteen hands high could easily walk under its neck; it seldom goes out of a walking pace, which is as fast as any other animals trot, and its legs are so long, that it could with ease step over a five barred gate, but its neck is so short that it cannot graze, but subsists by browsing, chiefly on the moose wood (whence it derives its name) neither can it drink in a standing posture, but is obliged to kneel for the water. The bark of the moose wood is so strong that the Indians use it for all sorts of purposes, it is an excellent substitute for rope and string, and is sometimes used by the settlers as traces for horses. The red deer are very numerous, and when fat generally weigh about two hundred pounds; from the month of August till Christmas they are good, and afford in the autumn excellent sport in hunting. When started by the dogs, they invariably fly to the nearest river or lake, where some of the party are ready with a canoe, so that when it plunges in the water, they may paddle after and shoot it. It is surprising that these deer are so numerous considering the quantity of wolves prowling about the forests.

There is an abundance of wild fruit, such as raspberries, strawberries and plums on the northern side of Upper Canada, the two first grow very plentifully and are excellent, the red raspberry equals in size and flavour that produced in England, yet might it be termed the weed of this country, the black raspberry makes an excellent preserve: there are also wild black currants which are very good, and gooseberries, but these are small and have no flavour: the currant is not a native of this country, but grows, when brought here to a large size. It is advisable for the emigrant to bring different kinds of fruit trees.

The wild pigeons, from May to August, are generally very numerous, and are excellent eating: they are about the size of the blue rock pigeon, and the cock-bird is much the same colour. Wild fruit is their principal food, but some seasons when they are very numerous, they consume a great deal of grain: they arrive in immense flocks and are supposed to come some thousands of miles, crossing lakes two or three hundred miles wide: such is the instinct of these birds, that after the first flock have remained about a month they leave for their nurseries, where they hatch their young, and are soon after succeeded by others in succession continuing thus throughout the season, following precisely the same course, though at an immense distance through uncleared forests, and over trackless lakes.

There are a great quantity of frogs in Canada; they are the best bait for fish that can be had, particularly the green frog. The bull frog is an extraordinary little animal, on account of the great noise it makes, which very much resembles the bellowing of a bull.

Many of the French Canadians eat this animal, which is found to be a wholesome and nutritious food, when people can banish their prejudices.

The mosquitoes are the most annoying of all insects; it is a small fly, very much resembling the gnat which is often met with in England; the sting is very sharp, and occasions a blister particularly to new comers; they generally come here about the middle of May, after they have remained unmolested for about a month, comes their natural enemy the musquito hawk, an insect resembling the hornet in shape, they pursue the mosquito incessantly and devour it, so that after this hawk appears, the mosquito is seldom very troublesome.

It is common where they are very numerous, to see a large smudge made in the farm yards, around which the cattle, (which are also greatly tormented by them) will arrange themselves in order to rid themselves of these annoying flies; and it is quite necessary, prior to retiring to rest, to make a smoke in doors, in order to eject them from the house.

It is highly gratifying to pay a visit to an industrious new settler, after he has been two or three years on his land,—to partake of his humble, yet wholesome fare, particularly should he be blessed with a help-mate, of those neat and cleanly habits, which always impart an air of comfort even to the most humble dwelling. See him at his morning meal,—the clean white deal table, the plentiful supply of ham, the ample dish of potatoes, the hearth-baked bread, the pitcher of new milk, the maple sugar, with the addition of tea; and with the exception of the tea, all the produce of his little new farm.

Unfortunately this is not always the case; people of indolent, dirty habits, are comfortable under no circumstances, and in no country; but if a man be only industrious, even if he have no knowledge of agriculture whatever, he must succeed; and every necessary comfort is within his reach.

In sailing down the river in the summer season, from the Chats to By-town, what numerous objects of interest present themselves,—to the rear are the beautiful falls at the Chats, its widely extended bays studded with islands; on one side are the bold heights covered with forest trees with their splendid foliage: on the other, and in the distance is seen the cragged tree topped mountain rearing its head above the clouds; in front appears the stately flowing stream, the Ottawa, with ever and anon the lightly, gliding, gay canoe; and every now and then a small opening discovers a neat little dwelling, with its curling smoke just emerging from between the trees.

All must acknowledge the beauty and sublimity of the Alps, the stupendous grandeur of Niagara, but the diversified and interesting scenery of the Ottawa must not be denied. The upper town of By-town contains many neat houses in the cottage style; there is one handsome stone building of large dimensions, with numerous out offices, the occupier of which deserves mention. He is a native of Ireland, and came a poor emigrant to Canada some eight or ten years ago: a year or two before the Rideau canal was made, he purchased a lot of land of one hundred acres for a very small sum of money, which is now the site of By-town, some of the government buildings, and a part of the canal. This person has already realized a handsome fortune; but by selling out parts of his land in building lots for short terms, he will, in a few years, be in the receipt of a considerable income arising from those rents. Upper By-town is at a very great elevation, overlooking an immense tract of land, and is perfectly distinct from the lower town, the canal passing between them, over which is now erected a neat stone bridge.

By-town is now quite a lively, fashionable place; here are to be seen the European fashions, silks vieing with muslins, the poke bonnet with the immense leghorn. Here are quadrille parties, and Scotch reel parties, and many other parties where mirth usually presides. There are now many respectable mechanics and tradesmen established here: emigration has in some degree flowed to this part of the Province for these last few years, and it has the appearance of much bustle and animation; from the great number of men employed on the canal by government contractors, it requires pretty strict discipline to keep them all in order,—there is something like a mutiny every now and then breaking out amongst them; and on the whole, Col. By has certainly no sinecure. The government pays three shillings a day to each man, on which they might live very well and save money, where provisions are to be bought so cheap as they are here; most of them have their own little cabins to live in, with a plot of ground to each, enough to grow potatoes sufficient for their own consumption, which is a consideration of some importance to them. Such a mart has By-town already, that in the winter, when sleighing is good, the place is thronged by the country people bringing their various produce to dispose of, and at this time of the year provisions are particularly cheap. Fresh pork at five or six dollars a hundred, beef at five dollars, mutton about three shillings a quarter, and poultry of all kinds very plenty and cheap. The living at taverns is high, considering the cheap rate of provisions: a dollar a day is the usual charge. There are abundance of them opened, but so few are kept in any decent order, that a respectable person cannot reconcile himself to their accommodations.

New houses are appearing in all directions about By-town, and the lands for some miles are gradually taken up and settled on. It is a matter of no ordinary difficulty after a lot of land in the bush has been purchased, to find out where it is situated; for tho' there are diagrams explaining the numbers and situation, with other particulars of the different lots, yet this lot might chance to be situated some eight or ten miles in the forest; and did there not happen to be settled every here and there a person well acquainted with the lay of the country,

omers would never of themselves be able to find
ut their different portions. They are all survey-
d, and posts are put up at the corners of the dif-
rent lots, denoting their numbers; but to an utter
ranger, these landmarks are of but little use, par-
ularly in trackless forests. The woods, even to
rsons who have long been settled in this coun-
y, are very treacherous, but not to the native born
merican, who seems to have a kind of instinct in
ding his way in the untrodden bush.

The success generally attending American set-
rs is in a great measure to be attributed to the
nner in which they are brought up by their pa-
ts, and their customs in this respect as regards
h sexes, are not altogether unworthy our imita-
: habits of practical industry are early instilled
he minds of the children, paying at the same
e a proper attention to an useful education; for
 evident that the schoolmaster has been, and is
 abroad in the United States: their manners,
 true, are not so polished,—there is not that
ward show of civility that is recognized in most
s of Europe; they have certainly their peculiar-
, strange expressions, quaint remarks, but so
 most other countries. In forming a criterion
he education of children, a due regard should
ad to the habits of the country in which they

are brought up; in Europe such is the refined state of society, and the superabundance of persons in the lower ranks of life, that the industry of the higher or even the middle classes are scarcely ever called into action; these ideas are often imported here, and their influence frequently incapacitates individuals, when left to provide for themselves, from using the proper means to obtain the comforts, or even the necessaries of life.

There is a great difficulty in procuring servants here, independently of the expense of keeping them; in fact, labour, be it of either sex, is the riches of this country, and persons coming out from Europe if they expect to succeed, must reconcile themselvs to it. The only servants a family man should hire, are men servants of *all* work, instead of women servants of *all* work. Some of the Canadians are extremely clever in turning their hands to almost any thing.

There is a system adopted in various parts of Canada, particularly in the neighbourhood of Montreal and other large towns, of letting farms out upon shares; gentlemen of opulence in the towns and other places very often let out their farms upon those terms, and it is a very good plan for a new comer to embrace these opportunities if he can; it gives him an experience in the custom of the country, and particularly if he have no property of his own, offers him the means of acquiring a little to commence with on his own account: the owner of the farm provides stock, farming utensils and seed to crop his land for the first year, there are no wages paid of course, the tenant does either by himself or with assistance, all the labor of the farm, in return for which he gets his half of the crop, half of the stock bred on the farm, (the original stock being retained by the owner,) this system is frequently of mutual benefit; farms are let in this manner from one to three years and so on. It is astonishing with what rapidity a man's stock might, with care and attention, accumulate in the course of a few years: as an instance, a man commenced with the following supply of stock; two ewes and a ram, one cow, one mare, and one sow, he neither killed or sold any of his sheep, and at the expiration of five years he had fifty three sheep; he had sold two horses and had three left, eight head of horn cattle, he had killed a good many pigs and had plenty remaining.

A farmer's life in Canada, admitting that he has his share of work, is not the most irksome in the world, and it leaves him plenty of time for recreation. His most busy time commences usually about the twenty-fifth of April, when the snow and ice are quite gone. He first begins to plough his land, and then to sow oats, barley, peas, and spring wheat if he should have occasion. Indian corn is the next crop, and this should be in by the fifteenth of May; lastly, potatoes, which, after all, are the most important. They are usually planted in hillocks, but often with great success in drills: in the neighbourhood of Montreal and other places, they are done with less expense in drills than hillocks; they are put into the land quicker, in the first place, and the plough will save hand-hoeing; they are also much more expeditiously got out of the ground with the plough. After the farmer has put in all his crop, he should then look well to his fences; for it is of no use to crop the land unless it is well fenced also, it being the custom in most parts of the province to let the horned cattle range in the woods all the summer. This may not be a good plan, still it is one of expediency, for many a new settler, who has a cow, has probably no pasture for her for the first year or two. The farmer's crop being all in the land, and his fences well secured, he may now rest a while from his labours; shoot pigeons, which are generally very plenty at this season of the year, fish, visit his friends, or amuse himself as best suits his inclination, till about the fifteenth or twentieth of July, then his hay is fit to cut. Hay should be mowed just as the flower is

**IMAGE EVALUATION
TEST TARGET (MT-3)**

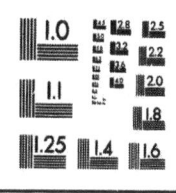

← 6" →

Photographic
Sciences
Corporation

23 WEST MAIN STREET
WEBSTER, N.Y. 14580
(716) 872-4503

leaving it; while the sap is yet full, it is the most profitable both for home consumption and for sale. It should, if possible, be cut one day, and housed or stacked the next; for if no rain occur, it will never heat. The idea of the sap causing it to heat, is all a chimera. It is a mistaken notion to dry hay too much in the sun; it is generally made here with little expense. Hay season over, in August his wheat and other grain begin to ripen, to get in which, will take him till September. The next grain that he has to look to, is his Indian corn, but that takes only a short time; the husks are merely torn off, and the stalks left standing, unless they are cut for fodder, for which they answer very well. In September the farmer ought to have his plough in his land, and before the latter end of this month, if possible, get in his fall wheat. Wheat sown in October generally does very well, and even in November; in fact, it is sometimes sown when the frost and snow have clotted the earth, so as to be hardly broken with the harrow, and has yet been a good crop; but this is neither so good nor safe a mode as preparing the ground in September. His harvest being done, and his winter crop sown, the farmer is not now greatly pressed for time; still, he may generally find something to do to keep him out of idleness. In October his potatoes will be fit to take out of the ground, when they should be either well secured in his cellar, root-house, or in pits in the field. A root-house is a very necessary place to keep vegetables in for winter consumption. It is a long room or hole dug pretty deep in the earth, a double tier of logs round the sides, the vacuity being well filled with earth, and also the roof well covered with a double layer of logs and earth, so as not to admit the least air or light. This precaution is necessary to keep out the frost, which is most penetrating. The extreme severity of the frost in Canada in the winter is almost incredible, for it frequently freezes the nose and ears. The usual method, when one person meets another in this predicament, is to take up some snow and rub the affeted part till is restored the circulation of the blood, for the frozen persons themselves feel no pain whatever. I have sat by the fire-side when, while the sap has been oozing out at the ends of the wood then burning in the fire, it has been instantly frozen hard. In taking tea, the cups, and saucers, tea-pot and all, frequently freeze to the table. However, with due precaution, potatoes and other roots and vegetables might be well secured through the winter. If the farmer have any new land to clear, October is a good time to begin to under-brush and chop; he can also spare a day

F

now and then for hunting, if his inclination be that way bent. In November he ought to look out for his winter's stock of fire-wood, which is a matter of some importance in Canada. It is by far the most desirable plan every year to lay up a year's stock of fire-wood before-hand, for green wood taken to burn, moulders away, and does not give that heat which is derived from wood that has been laid by for some time; the ashes that a family will make through the season, is of some consequence; a shed should be erected, not too near the dwelling, in case of fire, but at a convenient distance, to keep the ashes thoroughly dry, and many dollars would accumulate in the course of a year. In November, the snow usually commences, then the farmer has to look out for good winter quarters for his cattle, and also to see that his own dwelling is well tiled in, get all his vegetables out of the ground, and have a plenty of grain ground, for many of the mills are stopped during the winter months, from the severity of the frost. November is generally the slaughtering month; some sheep are killed, and are hung up to freeze for the winter supply, and pigs, beef, &c. December is frequently an open month, till Christmas, and the farmer might keep on with his under-brushing and chopping till after he has eaten his Christmas dinner. The snow getting sufficiently deep, and the rivers freezing hard, sleighing generally begins. Now is the time to get the sleighs and harness in proper order, or this is the season for the settler who happens to have no good summer's road to his residence, to take what produce he may have to spare to market.

The houses at this season of the year are kept very warm and comfortable, by means of stoves, particularly the large double ones. Those stoves are fixed so that one will warm two rooms, and the pipes are so arranged as to give considerable heat to the upper parts of the houses. In the lower province particularly, the houses in the winter are kept so hot, as to be almost suffocating, and frequently accidents occur from persons not being aware of the heat of their stoves.

In January the ice begins to be of a proper thickness to bear a load with safety. The method adopted here, in order to ascertain if it be of a proper thickness to bear a horse with sleigh and load, is to take a good sharp axe and to strike it into the ice with all your might at one single blow, and if you penetrate to the water, it is considered not safe enough to travel on with a load, but if no water gushes out, it might then be trusted. It is extremely pleasant to travel on the ice, the horses being well corked, will trot along at great speed, and with

F2

perfect safety; and where it happens to be a road well frequented, the tinkling of the bells, the speed of the horses, and the variety of the vehicles, give it an air of great gaiety. It is delightful to travel on the ice on a fine moon-light night; for although it freezes harder at night than in the day, yet from there being generally little or no wind, the cold is not nearly so much felt; the greatest danger is being caught in a snow-storm. It is a custom in the winter to make, or rather plant roads on the ice; it is done when the ice first takes, by collecting a quantity of green brush, the branches of the fir and cedar trees, making holes in the ice, and planting this brush in groves across the ice to any given place; it thus serves for a road all the winter. At different places, both on the St. Lawrence and on the Ottawa, you will see these roads continuing for miles, and are of the greatest utility. With the exception of travelling about, the farmer has little to do now, besides feeding his stock. Nothing is to be seen but the tops of the fences; and the buildings, and sometimes fences and all, are totally buried in the snow. Winter has now assumed her wonted stillness—all in the forest is silent as the tomb—not a bird—not a sound—not a creature, is now to be seen or heard—not even a leaf to rustle on the trees—it is now the midnight of nature's slumbers.

The farmers' occupation in February, will be found much the same as in the preceding month, attending his cattle, chopping fire-wood, and taking to market. Here it would be well to observe upon the prudence of the Farmers' keeping altogether out of debt with the merchants or innkeepers. It is too often the case with the young farmer to obtain goods upon the faith of his forth-coming crop. This is a system of thraldom that frequently keeps him in debt for years, for while he gets his supplies upon credit, there is not the same providential management over his out goings. But when a man takes no credit, but pays for his goods as he gets them, he will feel the necessity of keeping within due bounds, besides the consideration that at the end of seven years he will be a considerable gainer. For where he buys for the ready cash, he will purchase considerably cheaper.

March is reckoned the last month of sleighing, though the ice is generally good through the whole of this month; towards the latter end of March some remote symtoms of spring begin to develope themselves.

The severity of the winter now begins to relax a little. Passing through the Forests you will now and then hear a tree crack from the effects of the thaw, as if it were the report of a gun; this is the time to begin making sugar from the maple tree, when the sap first begins to rise. The ice on the river now gives way, and the confined air finding vent thro' the crevices of the thawing ice, explodes and produces a rumbling noise much resembling distant thunder. The cattle yet require their constant supply of fodder, for there is no green food for some little time yet, and when the snow leaves the grass it has at first a dead rusty hue, but when once vegetation begins to spring, the rapidity of change is beyond conception. Towards the middle of April the change in the season becomes visible, and the approach of spring is hailed with feelings of pleasure and delight. The plough and the harrow now begin to be thought of, and the farmer must make up his mind to labour and assiduity.

The manufacture of the maple sugar is very similar to the process of making potash, the one being by evaporation of the water from the ley, —the other by the evaporation of the liquid from the essence of the maple sap. Proportionable to the quantity of sugar intended to be made, a number of small troughs are prepared, each of which will collect sufficient sap in the season to make one pound of sugar. Those troughs are made simply by splitting a small tree and cutting it up into convenient lengths :—thus supposing it is intended to

CANADA AS IT IS.   73

make 200 pounds, of course so many troughs are provided; having collected the sap, which is done by placing a trough under each maple tree in which a notch is cut, out of which the sap oozes; a small flat stick is first placed to convey the sap into the trough, and every morning that it continues running it is collected and reserved in a large cask. Having collected the sap, boiling commences, and continues until it is reduced to the consistency of sugar.

There are two ways from By-town to Kingston; the one by the line of the Rideau canal; the other, which is now called the *old road*, by way of Richmond and Perth,—and through a line of tolerably well settled townships. Very soon after leaving By-town, on the Richmond road, evident characteristics of the establishment of a country recently called into existence by the hand of industry and perseverance, begin to make their appearance: the sturdy forest bends beneath the stroke of the vigorous axe,—the empire of solitude and silence yields up their dominion to life and animation,— and the hum of industry is heard.

Such, doubtless, was the state of our parent country, in the remote ages of the world; but to remain in the torpid state of nature could never be the intention of our Creator. He gives to his

F4

creatures a land for their inheritance,—but to man he says, " by the sweat of thy brow shalt thou eat bread ;" and we are not to confine the interpretation of this sentence to the literal tilling of the soil, but in its more general and extensive application. The means are given to man whereby he may convert the wilderness into a pleasant country,— whereby he may call into existence the hidden treasures of the earth,—render her the means of support to the present generation,—the reciprocal advantage to distant parts of the world.

Man was not sent into the world to be a useless being,—to eat the fruits of the earth with the view only to gratify his sensual appetite, but to be of service to his fellow-creatures,—to render his assistance to the general welfare of society,—to consider the wants of the community as the wants of himself,—to hold out by precept and example the practical good of enlarged benevolence.

Man neglecting to cherish and practice these ideas, too often relapses into a state of apathy and indifference,—his mind becomes corroded with selfish and contracted feelings,—he lives but to himself,—the mere being of existence.

Richmond, distant from By-town about twenty miles, is rather a swampy, low country: the road to it is distinguished for having many of those ribbed roads, called (not inaptly) corduroy bridges. Those bridges are sometimes a mile or two long. They are generally composed of logs of cedar laid parallel at the sides with the road, and other logs laid transversely, and resting their ends on the side logs. A few years ago this road, particularly near Richmond, was in such a state as to be scarcely passable; but within these three years it is very much improved, and still continues to be so; and for the traveller there is excellent accommodation.

The lands in the neighbourhood of Richmond, are some of the richest in the Province; but the situation being rather low and swampy, it is not considered so healthy as some other parts. The late Duke of Richmond unfortuuately lost his life within a few miles of this place, from the bite of a fox. He intended Richmond to have been a town of considerable importance; here are now to be seen the outlines of extensive streets, which were all regularly laid; numerous skeletons of large buildings are still standing; here was to have been a Cheapside, there a Ludgate Hill. Fleet-street at another place, and the Old Bailey crossing at right angles, with a Snow Hill in the centre,—though now *snow* hills are not wanting at this place in the winter.

Richmond is at the present time a place of considerable business, and the main thoroughfare through the heart of this part of Upper Canada. It will also be benefited materially by the accomplishment of the Rideau canal,—it will open a navigation to the Ottawa by means of the continuation of the York river, (upon which Richmond is situated) with the Rideau: thus the good effects of this great public work are felt more or less in all the surrounding country.

In going from Richmond to Perth, the traveller will pass through some rather thickly settled townships. The Rideau settlement, between Richmond and Perth, is one of the largest and best settlements within many miles; it owes its rise principally to the lumber trade on the Ottawa river. Before there were any settlements on or in the neighbourhood of the Ottawa, the supplies of fodder—hay, oats, &c., (required for getting out lumber) used to be drawn nearly all from the Rideau settlement, which at that time was their principal market.

The next township is Beckwith, which contains about two thousand inhabitants; among whom are many respectable Scotch families. Instances are not wanting in the township of persons who came out to Canada, not many years ago, with very scanty means, if any at all—who are now very comfortably situated, having good large farms, plenty of cows, sheep, horses, pigs, &c. &c., and living in a state of great respectability. And it may be observed, that wherever our northern brethren form settlements, there are to be seen their usual characteristics of industry, perseverance, and orderly conduct; they seldom fail in giving their children useful educations, which are the surest means of making them good members of society.

The only taxes known here at present, are the assess on property of one penny in the pound, which goes towards repairing the roads, and a half penny more to pay the sitting members of the House of Assembly. A man consequently having a farm of about fifty acres of cleared land, with stock, dwelling house, &c., pays on an average about a dollar and a half per year. On wild lands taken up, the assess is very trifling; but those who take up lands and neglect to improve them are liable to pay the assess on them. An act was passed in the House of Assembly in the Upper Province, that where parties neglected to pay the assessment on wild or any other lands, for eight years in succession, the sheriff of each district should be authorized to sell, annually, all such lands in arrear, redeemable by the original owners at any time within one year after the sale of such lands, by paying the purchaser the purchase money, for any improvement he might have made during the time of his possession, and twenty per cent. interest for his capital laid out. This act came into operation about a year ago, when the first sheriff's sale for arrears of assess took place; and in some remote parts these lands have been sold for a mere trifle—as little as three pence per acre. Thus two hundred acres of probably excellent land, (although in the wilderness,) for two pounds ten shillings currency.

The next township to Beckwith is Elmsley, which is also in a flourishing condition, containing about 1500 inhabitants, congregated from all parts of the British Kingdom. This district is remarkable for the number of deer seen from the road, frequently in herds of twelve or sixteen, which is unusual, as they seldom herd more than two or three together. In some particular spots there are what are termed deer licks: these are salt springs, of which these animals are so fond, that they flock to them from all parts of the forests, and are there shot in great numbers from a scaffold erected near the springs.

Perth is a well-built place; the houses are pretty regularly laid out, many of them large and handsome; the streets are also laid out uniformly. The court-houses and church are two spacious brick buildings; they stand on a hill of considerable elevation. Here are mills, stores, and plenty of good mechanics to supply the wants of the community.

Perth being the district town, commands great attention from all parts of the district of Bathurst, —in fact, it is quite the by-word, within a distance of fifty miles, if a person do not settle an affair or an account, "I will send you to Perth." There are many professional gentlemen, retired officers, &c., settled in and about the town; the society is respectable, and is remarkable for its sociability and gaiety. The taverns are superior to what might be expected from a comparatively small inland town.

Perth seems destined to become of considerable importance; its situation is immediately in the heart of a flourishing, well-settled part of the country, and it holds direct communication with two good inland rivers—the Mississippi and the Rideau; though the latter will ere long be converted into a source of navigation far superior to any thing contemplated when Perth was first settled. There is not an inland town more likely to derive greater advantage from the navigation of the Rideau canal, than Perth—with its gradual accession of settlers, the rapid opening of the country in its immediate neighborhood, and hence the improvement of the roads and means of communication. Independent of these considerations, so long as the judicial business of the district is transacted here, it must, in a great measure, be a place of pre-eminence. Such has been the increased settlement of the Bathurst district within the last ten years, that cases of some importance and magnitude are frequently brought before the judicial authorities at the Perth assizes. The young country is governed by a code of laws granted by its parent state, the fundamental principles of which breathe more of the true spirit of liberty to the subject, than any government on earth. But the greatest of all blessings to a British subject, is that safeguard of inestimable value to the protection of his person and property, and ever to be held one of her most sacred rights—namely, trial by jury. This is a right guarantied to every British subject,—a right that he watches over with as jealous an eye as the possession of his paternal estate. In fact, it is one of the principal compacts that binds king and people: it does unfortunately happen, that in some particular situations, persons are called on to exercise the all-important duty of jurors, who from former habits of life, or want of education, are rendered incapable of forming within their own minds correct ideas of the merits of various cases submitted to their consideration. Is it not doubtful whether there are not a class of men, who from the above causes are too often led astray by the sophistry of counsel on one side, and from an undue bias in their own minds on the other. The causes are not to be wondered at, if we consider for a moment the sphere of life, in which some persons who are now freeholders of the soil of Upper Canada have been brought up,— and their inabilities to discharge those functions; they themselves feel as acutely as any party; they have been reared by parents who are generally in too poor a condition of life to give them the least education, and whose utmost stretch is to be enabled to supply their families with food and clothing; their children are literally brought up in ignorance and darkness ;—and is it, then, suprising that this class of persons, (here metamorphosed into the freeholders of the soil,) should be incapable of performing duties requiring the aid of education, and the influence of admirable examples. There are, then, in this province some cases where persons are called on to exercise the important duty of watching over the lives and liberties of their fellow subjects, who, from their want of education, are wholly incapable of duly discharging those duties; however, it may be hoped, from the general encouragement given to education to the rising generation in this province, that there will soon be no room for complaints on this score.

A case was tried at Perth, not many years ago, of an assault that occurred somewhere in the district of Bathurst, committed on a person to whom the offender was under considerable obligations. The person on whom the assault was committed, was a man of opulence, the other a poor man. It was an outrageous and most unwarrantable offence; but the stumbling-block in this case was—the plaintiff was rich, and the defendant poor; and though *justice* truly can never see, yet it is much to be feared, that she sometimes endeavours to draw aside the *bandage*. In this case, twelve freeholders were summoned and sworn on the jury; the case being closed, and left by the highest authority in the hands of the jury for their verdict, there was an evident difference of opinion amongst them. Foreman—" Brother juryman, I think we we can soon come to a conclusion in this case—it appears to be clearly proved, that * * * very grossly assaulted * * *." Another juryman—" I perfectly agree with you, Mr. Foreman; it appears to me to be clearly made out;" but not another of these twelve men could or would come to the same conclusion. A juryman—" By J——s, what business have we to bother our brains about all that them there gentlemen has been talking about these two hours; all their larned sayings is no business of ours, and so it is'nt; sure, mus'nt we protect this poor man against the rich one? Suppose he did give the spalpeen a small taste of the shillalah, sure it will larn him how to behave in future." Foreman—" But, brother juryman, we are on our oaths, and it is our sacred duty to do justice." Juryman—" No more of your insinuations; if we was to send this poor man to prison, I should never forgive myself, and so I should'nt; and I say we have nothing to say against him." All the rest sturdily concurring in this opinion, the verdict was given in favor of the *aggressor*—I believe very much to the surprise of most present—for certainly in this instance, this invaluable bulwark of our liberties was most shamefully abused.

Perth, as centrally situated, ought to be considered as the district town for the several townships within its immediate range, such as Drummond, Beckwith, and many more; but it is extremely inconvenient and expensive to the inhabitants on and near the Ottawa, a distance of more than fifty miles, that they should have to travel thus far at all times of the year, to transact any petty law proceeding that calls for their personal attendance. By-Town ought certainly be made a separate district town, for that part bordering on and near the Ottawa. It is much to be desired that the present sitting member should use his influence in endeavouring to procure such a regulation; but in addition to the influence of the present member, the county of Carleton having by its now increased ratio of population, come up to the standard which gives a county the right of sending two members to the House of Assembly, by the next session, return two representatives to the Legislature of the Upper Province. The time of election is fixed for the early part of next winter. There are already two gentlemen come forward as candidates for the honor. The one is a son of Colonel Burke, a gentleman well known in the country, and who was very active in the first settlement of this part of the province; the other is Mr. Pinkey, a gentleman of independent property, now residing at March; it is therefore to be hoped, that with this accession of representative influence, the wants of every part of the county will not be forgotten. Perth is a town that seems to encourage within itself the means of its own improvement. It appears to contain a good share of public spirit, without which, every place, however advantageous in situation, soon sinks into insignificance. It supports a well circulated paper, called the "Independent Examiner and Bathurst District Advertiser."

Leaving Perth, you again plunge into the wilderness, but the axe is now so busy in this part of the world, that a visible change is constantly taking place. You see many little new shanties springing up in every direction, heaps of logs burning in one place, gangs of men and oxen logging in another, choppers busy in pursuing their laborious work, road makers engaged in rendering the muddy swamp passable, and probably here and there the newly arrived settler, together with his world's all, with a large storage of broken and half-broken furniture, at first lost in amazement at the extraordinary change, from his former scenes in life. These are some of the characteristics of the first settlement of a country, but as soon as the settler gets on his land, has his shantee erected, and made a little comfortable, a bit of land chopped, cleared, and under crop, his family all around him, and his wife reconciled, he soon gets familiar amongst his new neighbors, and with the roads in his immediate neighbourhood. He now begins himself to be thoroughly reconciled, and soon forgets most of

G

the little troubles and inconveniencies he has had to contend with.

After leaving Perth about ten or fifteen miles, the country begins to be remarkably well settled. There are some very large and good settlements, and the country gradually improves at the nearer approach towards Kingston, which is easily accounted for. The St. Lawrence side of the Upper Province has been partially settled for these forty or fifty years, and the tide of emigration has principally flown to this part of Upper Canada; for until these four or five years, the Ottawa was scarcely known, but to a few persons who dealt in furs, and to the officers of the Hudson's Bay Company. It is only within these twelve years that any settlement whatever was made on the Upper Canada side bordering on the Ottawa; these are the townships of Nepean, Goulborn, Hantty, March, Parbolton, Fitzroy, and others; the grand source of improvement has taken place within these five years in the cutting of the Rideau Canal, but on the other side, about Kingston, are now what is termed the *Old* Settlements of the country. There is yet a vast tract of land which appears to have been unnoticed by those who have had the management in first surveying and regulating the gradual settlement of the Upper Province. It must strike any person who has ever been in the interior of the country, say fifty miles above the Chats, and taking a westerly direction, that it would have been highly desirable to have opened this part of the Upper Province, considering that the population has increased so rapidly. Here are immense tracts of fertile lands, some of them of the best quality laying dormant. It will be argued that the Canada Company are now, and have been for some time past, opening and forming new settlements in the Huron tract; granted they are—but are they not beginning where they ought to leave off? the Huron tract is an insulated part of the Upper Province—its very extremity.

In settling a new country, those parts should be first opened where the means of communication are most convenient, and also the gradual opening of the country should be had in view, keeping the line of settlements as near together as the nature of the country will admit.

If the part of the province alluded to were surveyed and opened by commencing a good road, having its extremity on one end on the shores of Lake Ontario, and the other on the Ottawa river, it would tend rapidly to the opening and settling the very heart of the Province of Upper Canada; here would be a communication between two navi-

G2

gable waters of the first magnitude. The interests of the Canada Company are most intimately connected with the welfare and prosperity of the Province, and hence the necessity of their pursuing bold and straight forward measures in its settlement. It is useless to form a few small locations here and there in the remote districts, or to make partial roads; they should open a large tract of country at once, and that in the most desirable and central part of the Province. Wherever there are good roads, there will the settlers flock; but to offer lands for sale where there can be no means of communication, is to accomplish a very small portion of the good which is at their command. It may be asked, is not the country opened now from one extent to the other, by means of the Rideau Canal? But this is by no means the heart of Upper Canada; neither ought any public measure to stay the operations of the Canada Company in their systems of improvement. This immense work has been effected at the public expense, and the Canada Company are reaping the chief advantages by enhancing the value and expediting the sale of their lands in its immediate neighbourhood. Notwithstanding the large accession of settlers this season, and those to be expected in future, yet the Province will not be settled as it ought, unless more

CANADA AS IT IS.   89

liberal plans are adopted; the company themselves would reap tenfold advantages; for where they now dispose of one thousand acres of land, they might sell ten thousand. They are well aware that in a neighbouring country, lands are at all times to be had cheap, and there the means of communication are not neglected. Yonge street and other places might be instanced, but Yonge street in particular, and all the road to Penetanguishem. Some of the best settlements in the Province are on this road, and in its vicinity. The reason is obvious: it is not because the lands are the best; for a considerable distance they are very poor and sandy; but even here they are well settled. Persons would rather, and it is better for them to locate on ordinary lands, where there are good roads and means of communication, than on the very best soils, where those conveniencies are not to be found. In remote and isolated situations, land is scarcely worth accepting.

The Canada Company is composed of a body of men (the shareholders in London and elsewhere,) who are utterly incapable of forming a just opinion of the nature and local wants of this country. Their capital is invested, and all they look to is a return of interest, without duly considering the nature of the undertaking in which their capital is

G3

engaged, or the means most proper to be adopted for the furtherance of its prosperity. They know that land is land any where, and they think that it is only to offer it for sale to get purchasers. Whether the policy is a good one or not, of ever having delegated to any body of men the control over such a vast tract of territory, where the welfare and interests of so large a body of his Majesty's subjects are so intimately connected, *time best will tell.*

On the approach to Kingston, the country is much settled by natives from Ireland, and here the character of the Irishman may be seen to advantage; he is generally hardy, patient, industrious, and not intimidated at trifles, and gets over his first difficulties very well; he is likewise a quiet peaceable neighbour and a good subject, when his passions are not inflamed with liquor, or his feelings worked upon by the designing, and in this distant land, how much is it to be lamented, that the causes which produce most of the feuds and heart-burnings in their own country should be kept up and cherished here. If there be the shadow of a pretence for these most invidious party feelings at home, surely here they are altogether inexcusable and criminal. Whether it be on the one side or on the other, whether these fends and party animosities have been cherished by the Irish Protestant or by the Irish Catholic, let them be banished altogether from this hitherto unpolluted soil.

The country around Kingston is distinguished by an evident superiority of the state of agriculture, here they are large growers of that staple commodity of consumption and commerce, wheat, a grain that as long as England continues her present policy towards this Country cannot be too much encouraged, not only for exportation home will it be wanted; but also for the supply of the northern river, for there they are only just now emerging from the wilderness; if they can raise an acre or two each kind of grain, it is as much as they can do for the first few years. Wheat is certainly the best grain grown in Upper Canada, for while both barley and oats somewhat degenerate, wheat at lest equals if not rather excels the English growth.

Kingston is now fast recovering from the severe check given to her commercial prosperity a few years ago: she is now re-establishing herself upon a firm basis, and from her central situation cannot, as long as the Province continues to flourish, fail to be a town of considerable importance. The Rideau canal has been of the utmost consequence to the town; and she is likely to derive as much or more advantage from its navigation than any other place in the Province;—it will be the principal depot at the head waters of the canal,—taking in and storing all the produce that will pass through —coming down from York, Niagara, and all places above, and through the Welland canal. There can be no question but Kingston will ultimately be one of the first towns in Upper Canada. It now exceeds any other in population,—it commands a delightful view of Lake Ontario,—the steam-boats passing and repassing between Prescot and Niagara, all making the port of Kingston in their way, renders it in the summer a place of very considerable importance and activity. The troops more or less permanently stationed here, likewise contribute to its gaiety.

The site of Kingston is most judiciously chosen; it is built on the curve of the Bay. On the opposite side stands the Garrison, commanding the entrance to the town; it altogether presents a formidable front, and is a plan that would put to the test the strength of any enemy. The streets which are numerous are regularly laid out, butting on the Bay, and generally uniform and well built.

Kingston and the surrounding country, like every other part of the Province, are now beginning to feel the beneficial effects of the judicious system of policy under which the Canadas have for the last few years flourished. Prior to this period the agriculture, and consequently the commerce of the country were in a drooping state,—the farmer received no price for his produce to stimulate him to exertion,—he could ill afford to purchase any thing beyond the bare necessaries of life, and hardly those; the storekeeper's stock hung heavy on his hands; hence the want of punctuality in fulfilling his engagements with the merchant, and the general want of confidence through the whole commercial body. No place felt the effects from those causes more severely than Kingston. It might be said, why should this country look to England for support and protection to her agriculture and commerce?——for the very strongest grounds. She is a body politic as well as a colony,—a part and parcel of the British Empire. She can pass no laws of herself, with regard to her foreign policy; but as a colony, is of course under the guidance and direction of laws emanating from her parent state.

Is Canada, when kept in this state of cruel depression, likely to be productive of those real and solid advantages to her parent state which her now prosperous condition would warrant us in anticipating. A pampering and unsettled policy really operates in a cruel manner towards a young and rising country;—for a few years she fancies herself in established prosperity,—the man of laudable ambition and enterprize embarks his capital in undertakings of magnitude,—the agriculturist goes on with spirit and energy in improving and cultivating the soil,—the commercial character speculates upon what he reasonably considers a firm basis,—the united prospects of every class flourish for perhaps three or four years, when a new regulation is issued that gives an immediate check to industry, ruins commerce, and locks up the very channels of enterprize to every class of persons.

Canada wants a regular settled system of policy, that she may calculate with some degree of certainty upon the returns she is likely to get for her various surplus produce. Without this she must ever remain in that feverish uncertain state too often observable in the general commerce of this country.

Kingston has to boast of some establishments in its neighbourhood of the first consequence; these are the Marmora Iron Works carried to a considerable extent, and produce some wares, which for texture and quality will bear comparison with many imported articles of a similar fabric. There are the Gananouque Mills, so celebrated for the superior quality of flour they manufacture; and many other establishments in the vicinity of this important place place, equally deserving of notice.

On proceeding from Kingston to York, you keep in view of Lake Ontario most of the way, and have to pass through many very pleasant villages, with good inns, affording excellent accommodations. Their customs resemble in a great measure the manners of their opposite neighbours: for instance, whether it be at breakfast, dinner, or supper, they rarely spread the table, without putting on an ample supply of preserves, such as peaches, plums, apples, &c.

The first village of any consequence, after leaving Kingston, is Cobourg,—a place newly sprung up; and a most delightful little village it is,—sloping down to the very water's edge. The houses all nearly new, clean, and well-built, mostly surrounded with tastefully laid out gardens, with the neat church topping the hill. The whole village from the lake has a most enchanting appearance; the inhabitants, too, are quite of the respectable order,—indeed, they pique themselves on keeping their society select.

There are many very extensive farmers in the neighbourhood, who cultivate very large tracts of land. Some of these agriculturists will transport in the course of a season two thousand bushels of wheat, or upwards. The country is pretty well settled for forty miles back, and still fast increasing. It must be acknowledged, that the manner of managing their farms is a model for many other parts of the Province; they seem to adopt the right system of tillage, not merely scratching over the land, and just dropping in the seed, (as is the custom in many parts of the Province,) but properly and effectively breaking up the soil with the plough, in a thorough husbandry-like manner. It is not the quantity sown to be considered, but the principle thing is the state and tillage of the land. At least one-third of the land in this Province is lost, through a bad system of tillage. The best crop that a farmer can have, who is poor and has not the means to well dress his land, is Indian corn. This is a grain that might be just dropped in the earth, and as fast as it grows, the hoe will perform the necessary tillage; it will succeed well in the same land for twenty years successively; and it generally finds a ready market. The seed that is necessary to plant a large breadth of Indian corn, is of no moment, consequently, should the crop fail, the loss is not felt. There are other kinds of produce that might

CANADA AS IT IS. 97

be raised with advantage, principally by hand labour. Hemp, for instance, is an article much wanted in this Province; still the growth of hemp is certainly attended with some expense, and perhaps not within the reach of every one. But there is another produce of great importance to every farmer who has any stock,—a crop which appears to be much, if not altogether overlooked in this country, which is carrots; they are amongst the best and most nutritious food for horses; one bushel of carrots will yield more nourishment than two bushels of oats or potatoes; and it is a remarkable fact, that horses will frequently leave oats to feed on carrots, after they have acquired a relish for them: generally other cattle as well as horses are fond of them, and thrive astonishingly well, when fed on them. They not only make them in good condition, but give them fine glossy coats. If farmers would turn their attention to raising this vegetable extensively, they would find an immense saving in grain, as well as a visible change in the thrift of their animals. As a matter of economy and profit, it is of vast importance. The quantity of carrots which may be raised from one acre of good land, is almost incredible: when the land is rich and mellow, an acre will yield from one to two thousand bushels; the process is simple, and the labour comparatively light;—select a rich piece of ground, tolerably dry, and as free from weeds as possible: plough it deep, make it mellow, and harrow it smooth; then sow your ground with the usual quantity of flaxseed, and harrow it in; after this sow about a quart of carrot seed to the acre, and brush it lightly,—both seeds will come up together; but the flax springing up with considerable rapidity, will so shade the carrots, that they will not gain much size till the flax is pulled. The shade of the flax will also prevent the weeds from growing, so as to interfere with the carrots. After the flax is pulled, which will be in July, the carrots will begin to flourish; especially if the weeds have been kept in check by the shade; for the pulling of the flax will so loosen the earth around them, and so expose them to the rays of the sun, as to give them new vigour and strength; at that time, also, the weeds will not grow rapidly, if at all. Thus may be raised two valuable crops, without impoverishing the land more than by a crop of corn or oats. It is not probable that the first attempt will yield so largely as has been suggested above, but if the proper precautions be taken, and are tolerably successful, one acre will produce about one thousand bushels of carrots, worth—

1 shilling per bushel,   £50 00
300 lbs. flax, worth 4d per lb.   5 00
    6 bushels flaxseed, about   2 00

To what use can an acre of land be applied by which it will produce half the amount? This may seem a large estimate, but it is, nevertheless true; and if any one wish to test the matter, let them try it next season. Horses will work on carrots as well as on oats, and keep in much better order. The above might probably be considered experimental farming; but in farming as well as in other matters, experiments have brought to light many valuable discoveries; in gardening in particular, and in all botanical researches, which to husbandry are nearly akin, to what amazing perfection the system of gardening is brought at home; and yet no further back than the reign of Queen Elizabeth, Holland furnished us with *green peas*, and even *potatoes*. But men generally do not relish the idea of going out of their regular track; they consider that to stoop to advice is beneath their notice, and hence they plod on in their own unprofitable way for the want of a more enlightened and productive system.

All the steam-boats navigating Lake Ontario, both up and down, touch at Albany, which renders it a village of some importance.

On leaving Cobourg, you pass on the high road leading to the capital of Upper Canada, the country is in many places along the line of this road still a wilderness; here and there are some good clearances, but they are not general till near *Port Hope*, which is sixty miles below York. This is another village similar to Cobourg, but not so large: it also butts on Lake Ontario, over which it has an extensive view. Port Hope contains at present about forty or fifty dwellings, and is now one of those pretty pleasant country villages so often to be met with.

Leaving Port Hope you now soon arrive at what might be termed the Yorkshire of Upper Canada; for here are the towns of Darlington, Scarborough, Harrowgate, Whitby and Pickering, and a township called Scarborough; and these places are settled very much by natives from Yorkshire. Many of the Upper Canada loyalists have settled on and about Scarborough. Doubtless the term is generally understood; they are persons from the United States, originally from British parents, who at the time of the American war, would not, from conscientious motives, take up arms against their original country and kindred. They withdrew from the States, and placed themselves under the protection of the British govern-

CANADA AS IT IS. 101

ment, who as a recompense for the sacrifices they had made, gave them grants of lands iu the Canadas, and also to their children.

When within about six miles of the town of York, it presents a very good and extensive view of it, stretching itself along the beach, on the northwest side of the harbour. . In the distant view, and commanding the entrance to the harbour, is the garrison, which has a very formidable appearance. The suburbs are marked by all those characteristics observable in the vicinity of most large towns at home. Dotted here and there are neat pretty villas, built on a handsome construction, having those compact little paddocks and shrubberies which so much adorn the country-house.

The first structure that engages the attention, is the new, handsome, and substantial wooden bridge built over the river Don. In the entrance to the town as well as this, many other handsome and useful buildings which now ornament it, was completed under the direction of the present excellent Governor Sir John Colborne.

The next building of any consequence is the large brick Catholic Church, a most substantial edifice. A distinguishing feature in the town of York is the numerous substantial brick dwelling-houses. The town is laid out with numerous streets butting on the lake shore, and crossing transversely the main street at right angles, called King-street; which runs in a straight line through the heart of the town, for a mile and a quarter in length. Here is a Newgate-street and a Cheapside, a Poultry, and Snow Hill, and many other names familiarly known in the British metropolis. Here is also another singular accumulation of names; for on the whole side of one street,t he inhabitants which comprised only two names, (Armstrong and Rideau.)

There are a great number of stores in York, and some of them are really elegant, and well supplied with the choicest wares manufactured in Europe. They all appear to do a great deal of business. York is altogether a place of extensive trade with the western part of the Upper Province; and the thickly settled townships surrounding it, is in fact the bay to this important part of Upper Canada. It is astonishing in the time of sleighing in the winter, when the roads are good, to see the number of large sleighs, with wheat and various kinds of produce, coming into the town; and it is altogether a very novel sight. Sometimes will be observed fifteen or twenty of those large box sleds, some drawn by two horses, others by four, all at full trot with their bells jingling, some driven by jolly looking Quakers, some by the singular sect called Tankards, who never shave their beards,—these growing nearly down to their middles, and with their little skimmer hats and long coats, have a most extraordinary appearance.—Then comes an Indian, with his well known dress, the universal blanket, driving in a load of frozen deer to market,—next a Yankee, with his load of frozen pigs, all as stiff as the shafts of his sleigh, himself dressed in his homespun suit of brown,—all these characters form a very striking contrast. The quantity of wheat deposited in York during the winter is very great; many of the principal storekeepers of the town purchasing very largely of this commodity. A large body of the farmers in Yonge-street, and in the townships in the vicinity of York, have adopted the plan of storing their own wheat; they have formed themselves into an association, and have built a very large storage at York, on the margin of the lake, where they store it in the winter, while the roads are good, and transport it down in the Spring,—thus securing to themselves the best prices. They have their secretary in York to see to the storage, and keep the account of deposits, &c.

H

The public market of York is uncommonly well supplied daily with fresh meat, poultry, vegetables, butter, cheese, &c. both in summer and winter. The present market house, which is extensive, appears scarcely large enough to accommodate the inhabitants of this fast increasing town. A contract has been made for the erection of a new market-house, and it is stated, that the estimated cost of the building will be about six thousand five hundred pounds currency. The prices of meat generally in the York market is, for beef about three pence per pound; mutton four pence; veal the same; a fat goose for two shillings; turkeys three and sixpence to five shillings; fowls nine pence to one shilling and six pence; butter eight to ten pence; cheese five pence.

York is also at some seasons of the year well supplied with fish taken in the lake. The salmon is excellent, and in great plenty. The lake salmon does not quite equal in flavour that taken in salt water. The colour is not so bright, but the fish are equally large, and very good eating. They are not caught in nets, but with the spear; the fisherman goes out at night in canoes or boats, keeping a light in the bow, which attracts the fish, when they are struck with the barbed spear, and easily secured. The lakes produce another very excellent fish, called white fish, generally of about three or four pounds weight; also the blue backed herring, much larger than the common herring, but of the same species. It is somewhat like the fresh herring, but rather of a milkish flavour. In fact, the most of those fish in the lakes are migraters from the sea; and there is no doubt, if the sea-fish could be introduced into the lakes, but they would breed and thrive in fresh water.

A gentleman of Upper Canada has proposed to the House of Assembly to vote the sum of five hundred pounds, to be appropriated to the purchase of all kinds of live sea fish, lobsters, oysters, and all descriptions of shell as well as other sea-fish, to be deposited in the lakes, for the purpose of trying the experiment of raising an inland supply. The various descriptions of herring (known to be natives of the sea)—flourish in these waters. There can be no reason why other natives of the same element should not also succeed, at least, it is not improbable. They now have a supply of fresh cod and oysters at York in the winter, but they are brought a distance of six or seven hundred miles, and of course the price is proportionate.

York is fast becoming a place of considerable importance. The situation is central, between a

H2

great extent of inland navigation and a very large tract of well settled country. All the supplies, for above a hundred and fifty miles above it, are drawn from York. There are already many considerable establishments in its neighbourhood, such as paper makers, hatters, parchment makers, potteries, and many other branches; and the mechanics generally, in and about York, are the most ingenious and best in the Province, and are here very numerous.

The grist-mills in the vicinity of York, too, deserve notice; they are upon a most ingenious and effective construction; they are after the American model, and are certainly the most simple, effective, and expeditious in their operations. It is not the custom here for millers to measure in the wheat they purchase, but to weigh all at the rate of sixty pounds to the bushel. The mills receive the wheat at the weighing machine; it then passes on in a trough worked by cogs, placed in rollers; then by conductors,—(these are a kind of leather pouch, each holding about a pint)—it is taken up to the smut machine, then to the fanning mill; from thence down to the grinding stones; up again by conductors to be bolted; from thence it passes into the large receiving bin, and into the barrels.— Thus the wheat is taken in at the weighing machine, passes through all these evolutions; and from the time of its being weighed till it is fine flour, and in the barrel, no hand touches it: it is all done by a simple piece of machinery. Flour and wheat are articles of considerable trade at York. Salt is another article of importance; and nearly, if not quite all, the salt that passes through the hands of the merchants at York, is imported from Onondaga in the States, where it is made. The amount paid to the Americans, for this single article, in the course of a year, must be some thousands of pounds. There are the same facilities for manufacturing salt in some parts of the Upper Province, which they have in the inland part of the States—namely, salt springs: but who is to advance the necessary capital, in this Province, required to carry on such works? We have no banks here to assist us. Thus thousands are annually spent in the Province, both for this and many other necessaries.

The inns and other places of accommodation are very numerous in York; and some of them are kept in the best order, and on a very large scale. There are likewise many private boarding-houses, equal, if not superior, to any in the Province; and the charges, considering the nature of those accommodations, very reasonable. Many of the taverns are kept by Americans.

It is no uncommon thing in taverns in the States to find a Bible placed in each bed-room, for the use of visiters; and some of these taverns will supply no liquors, on Sundays, to any persons but those really travelling; and a very excellent and proper regulation it certainly is.

The arrival of the numerous emigrants at York, during the summer, is a source of great profit to the tavern-keepers. In fact, many of them loiter at these houses much too long for their own interest. The numerous groups of emigrants collected on the beach, immediately after the arrival of a steam-boat, is a scene of no common interest, and exhibits a very singular taste in the ideas of economy. You will see, probably, a few old chairs not worth half a dollar each, which have been brought nearly or quite five thousand miles; with old bedsteads, and other pieces of common furniture, that could have been disposed of at home for nearly as much as new would cost here; for wood being so very abundant in Canada, these common articles of furniture are very cheap in most parts of the Province; very good common chairs, quite new, are to be bought for four or five shillings each, and sometimes less; but the people at home imagine there are no persons here who can manufacture these kind of things. In this they are much mistaken; for such is the accumulation of furniture for sale in the Upper Province, that the body of cabinet makers of York, during the last session of the Assembly, petitioned the House to pass an act prohibiting the importation of furniture from the United States; therefore, emigrants should not bring any lumbering heavy furniture with them to this country.

The navigable part of the emigrant's long journey generally ends at York; and here are to be seen groups of men, women, and children, each betraying, in their countenances, marks of the unsettled state of their ideas in this, to them, strange country. Some are anxiously seeking their friends; some are inquiring for the most eligible situations to settle in; others are endeavouring to procure present employment: and many are the dupes of unprincipled characters, who, for the sake of plundering these poor strangers, often lead them into situations the most inimical to their interest.

The trades of York appear to be more distinctly classed than are to be observed in many other towns in Canada. There are drapers who appear to keep only those peculiar kind of goods in their immediate line, denominated dry goods. Here are grocery and spirit stores, selling nothing but heavy kinds of goods, spirits, and wines. Whiskey is an article to be had exceedingly cheap, as low as one shilling and six pence a gallon: cider, too, is very cheap—at about three pence per gallon, and very good. There are in York ironmongers, silversmiths, druggists, stationers, &c., who respectively seem to confine themselves to the sale of their legitimate articles of trade.

The suburbs of York are remarkable for the rich appearance of its numerous gardens, which exhibit the evident marks of a congenial climate. Apples, particularly, thrive in the greatest luxuriance. Most kinds of fruit and vegetables seem to flourish here; the red currant and the plum grow to a very great size; cabbages, celery, cauliflowers, and in fact all kinds of culinary vegetables, are raised here in the greatest abundance. They have here a pea called the six week pea, which is planted and comes to maturity in six weeks. Many fruits and vegetables are raised in Upper Canada which will not come to perfection at home, at least not in the open air. Melons are here planted openly in the gardens, or in the fields; indeed, they succeed best on a spot where a log heap has been burnt. Cucumbers also grow to an uncommon size when planted in the same spots. They are also much better than those grown in Europe. If some kinds of garden seeds are sown here in the fall of the year, they succeed well; and persons would profit much by adopting this system—of sowing onions, carrots, parsnips, and asparagus, and other kinds of the hardy plants, that frost will not injure. Seeds, by being sown in the fall of the year, acquire an early growth in the Spring, and get strong before the grub attacks them.

About fifty miles above York, towards the Western District, and at Niagara, which is thirty-six miles across the lake, peaches grow in the greatest abundance, on trees planted in the gardens or orchards, just the same as the apples. They are not so large as those raised on wall trees, nor have they the same rich appearance; they are green when ripe, but are very sweet and good,—are used in great quantities for preserving, and are also made into peach brandy. They are brought from Niagara to York in very large boat loads, and sold out of the boats at the wharf side, at sometimes a shilling, and even as low as six pence a bushel.

The harbour of York presents a scene of great interest when the navigation of the lake is open. Her placid waters being the receptacle of a great variety of craft,—light fancy painted skiffs, some for pleasure, some for business, a numerous anchorage of sloops freighted with a variety of produce; one handsome steamer, just departing; another of portentous dimensions, just now seen in the offing,—regarded with an anxious eye by the groups of characters walking to and fro on the long extended wharf. The whole scene presents to the view an interest not easily conceived.

There have been for the last two or three years, three large steam-boats running constantly between Prescott and Niagara,—the splendid new steamer, the Great Britain, now makes the fourth. Niagara is merely the nominal place of destination. The steam-boats generally land four fifths of their cargoes and passengers at York. The Canada runs every morning to Niagara, and returns the same afternoon. There is also another at the head of the lake, taking passengers and loading for Hamilton, Dundas, Ancaster, and all parts of the west.

The improvements in the town of York are making inconceivable progress. Both public and private buildings, of the most substantial kind, are being erected in all directions. They are mostly of brick, of which article there is now an immense quantity made near the town. Mechanics of all grades obtain ready employment. The supplies of lumber and other building materials are not more than commensurate with the demand. In fact, the prosperity and growth of the capital seems to keep pace with the general improvement of the Province.

The large handsome brick buildings, now nearly completed, immediately opposite the lake, reflect the greatest credit on those engaged in their erection. These buildings are intended for the sittings of the Houses of Assembly, and the legislative body; and also for the occupation of some of the public offices. The government here appears to be concentrating the public offices under the same roof,—a most desirable regulation; for at present they are distributed all over town; and after a person has transacted business at one office, it takes him half a day to find out the next. The Government House, (the present residence of Sir John Colborne,) is a large white painted building, immediately in the rear of the building just alluded to. It altogether occupies about four acres of land, comprising a shrubbery, garden, &c. A sergeant's guard is always in attendance, and due military etiquette is observed. The greatest urbanity and attention is shown to all applicants on business, without distinction.

Facing the Government House is the new College of Upper Canada, comprising a large extent of buildings. The present number of scholars is about two hundred. There are three classical masters—two writing masters—a drawing and French master, with a few assistants. The establishment of this college is of the most incalculable advantage to the residents in and near York, and of Upper Canada generally; for here they have the means of giving their sons a liberal education for a comparatively trifling expense, the whole of the college fees not amounting to more than eight or ten pounds a year.

Near the college stands the hospital, a large commodious building, well adapted for the purpose for which it is intended.

There are many elegant private residences in the vicinity of York, built in a style that would do credit to any place in Europe. The jail and court-house are built in a manner that renders them an ornament to the body of the town. The House of Assembly is at present held at the court-house. It consists of about fifty members—attorneys, doctors, farmers, merchants, &c.

The place where they now hold their sittings, is in an immense room about eighty feet in length by forty in breadth. There are three or four anti-rooms for the accommodation of committees, &c. The room of sitting is fitted up with every convenience for the accommodation of the members. Each member has a desk, enclosing a secretaire for the deposite of his letters and papers. At the extremity of the room is an elevated throne under a canopy; above which are his Majesty's coat of arms. The throne is occupied by the speaker, who sits in his robe of office and shovel hat. There are the mace bearer, sergeant-at-arms, usher of the black rod, &c., all in attendance. There is also an elevated enclosure for the accommodation of the gentlemen of the press.

The House usually sits from the beginning of January to the middle of March. At the opening of the session, the Governor goes in state to the House in a similar form to that observed by the King at home—being here his representative.

The bank of York is a large handsome building, entered by a flight of stone steps; having doors, and the fittings up in the inside, of mahogany. The business, which is now very considerable, seems to be conducted with great regularity and despatch. There are no lack of professional men in York, having a considerable number of lawyers and doctors. The periodical publications appear to be very well supported in the town and its vicinity. There are five regular weekly papers, besides the Government Gazette—these are the Courier, the Colonial

Advocate, Canadian Freeman, Observer, and the Christian Guardian. The price of papers in Canada is generally four dollars a year.

There is great encouragement for mechanics in and about York. The wages of smiths and carpenters are seven shillings and six pence a day; masons about the same. Most other trades are well paid. They certainly may live very much cheaper here than at home; and if they are sober men, they have a chance of saving money. Shoe makers, hatters, and tailors, get the highest wages in York, for such is the gaiety of this thriving town, that their respective trades are well encouraged. Here are advertising boot makers from " Hoby's," tailors from " Bond-street," and milliners and dress makers from the " West End;" in fact, here is a London in miniature. The place is yet too small to support a regular theatre; although they have occasionally some travelling performers. The gaiety of York is developed in their private parties, which is greatly enhanced by the beauty and vivacity of the fair sex.

The religious sects are of many denominations, —the Roman Catholics, Presbyterians, Methodists, Congregationalists, and Episcopalians; and whatever they might be in other parts of the Province, the latter are the most numerous in the capital.

The site of York is admirably chosen, as far as regards its convenience for the navigation of Lake Ontario; possessing a safe, commodious, and capacious bay, securing to craft of every description a safe anchorage. The lands, also, on the western side of the town, are high and dry, and admirably adapted for building, but there is a great drawback on the score of its unhealthiness of situation on the eastern side of the town, which, it is much to be feared, is irremoveable. At the head of the bay, which comes to the east side of York, are some very extensive stagnant marshes; they extend for six or seven miles; and are considered to be the principal agents in germinating the local diseases felt more or less in and about the town.

In Reesorville are two good taverns, two or three smiths, carpenters, a saddler, tailors, shoe makers, a regular post-office, several stores, and a church is now being built.

These little new villages, built up in the centre of the forest, have a most extraordinary appearance to any person who has been familiar with European towns. There, the immense space of surrounding country, all open to the view, is generally seen: here is, as it were, a town fenced in by an interminable forest.

A person travelling through the bush, feels much about the same sensation as he would, were he to be travelling through any part of the United Kingdom, with a bandage over his eyes, and only having it released upon his coming to any town or village. He is not always lonesome on his way; he sometimes may see a deer crossing his path; or the red or black squirrel playing in the trees; and peradventure he might meet with a bear.

Birds are seldom to be seen much in the heart of the forest, with the exception of the solitary woodpecker. The feathered tribe generally appear to be of a social habit; in the clearances, and near the villages they appear to be most at home. The inhabitants in this neighbourhood derive a great advantage from the abundance of salmon in the river Ruish, a small stream communicating with Lake Ontario. Each family in the Spring obtains enough to supply them for many months.

Further on in this direction of the country, lie the thriving townships of Brock, Innisfil, and others. Lands about these townships are to be had cheap, and consequently a desirable place of settlement for the emigrant who has but small means; and the roads, all through this part of the country to York, are good.

On the Yonge-street, about eighteen miles from York, are the very high lands, called the Oak Ridges; they extend for some miles, and are nearly all sandy and poor. But from hence upwards, the soil is of the most fertile description. On the top of these Ridges, is a lake of about a mile in circumference, and said to be twenty or thirty fathoms in depth. A few miles beyond them is the settlement of the curious sect called Tankards. They are dissenting Quakers; they do not marry; their dress is a long suit of home-spun brown cloth; they do not shave their beards, and altogether exhibit a most singular appearance.

A few miles from hence is the town of Newmarket, a place of importance in this part of the country. Newmarket comprises about a hundred houses; it is situated in the heart of a rich productive country, and is a place of great business of various descriptions. Here are two excellent gristmills; besides saw-mills, a hat and chair manufactory, which are very extensive; and a cloth or carding mill. The texture of the cloth made at this mill is of a fair quality; and the farmers in the neighbourhood have only to dress and prepare their wool a little, when it is taken to the mill, and is returned a good serviceable cloth.

Newmarket is quite a manufacturing town, upon

a small scale. Here is a large fur establishment, where they carry on an extensive trade in furs with the Indians about Lake Huron, and further northward. Here may be occasionally seen a body of Indians; they are very large, being on an average at least seven feet high; and their limbs are in proportion. These are entirely devoid of clothing, and their arms are certainly as large as the fore leg of an ox. They are part of a tribe of Indians, inhabiting the country about the Rocky Mountains, ten or fifteen hundred miles from hence. They were at war with a neighbouring tribe, who, notwithstanding their gigantic size, appear to have been more than a match for them, for the last party seen at York were a few, deputed by their tribe, to come down with the view of soliciting the assistance of the government against the hostile tribes. The government of course refused to interfere, and they were obliged to return to their own regions. They appear to be possessed of great strength and agility; they can run as fast as a middling horse can gallop.

All kinds of produce are raised in great plenty in the vicinity of Newmarket. They are remarkable here for the extremely fine quality of their honey; it is quite equal to the Narbonne honey, so celebrated in Europe.

The next place, five miles beyond Newmarket, is one of the most interesting little villages in the whole Province. From the peculiarity of the sect, the *Davidites*, or *Children of Peace*, as they call themselves, who inhabit it, and to whom it belongs, it is generally called the Village of Hope. Some call it David's Town, from the name of its founder, David Wilson, who is still living, and the head of this sect. The road from Newmarket to David's Town lies in a zigzag direction, and the village opens abruptly to the view, which gives it a peculiarly striking effect. Its site is most picturesque, being situated on the declivity of a hill of considerable elevation. The village is composed of about forty or fifty remarkably neat, clean dwellings; but what gives the most imposing effect is, the handsome newly built temple, which is built nearly on the summit of the hill, and is now nearly finished. It is intended for their public worship, and is built somewhat after the manner of Solomon's Temple. It is of a pyramidical form: the extreme height is about eighty feet; length and breadth of base about seventy feet,—contracting in elevation. It is decorated at the top with a gilded ball. The whole is of wood work, and painted white. The fitting up of the interior does them much credit. There is a handsome pulpit;

I

also an orchestra for the musicians, and their singing virgins, and every accommodation that can be desired. The building and finishing of this temple have been accomplished wholly by themselves. This sect lives in a little community, entirely to themselves. All matters of dispute arising between them are referred to David; he was their founder; he is now their director and lawgiver: all their produce passes through his hands. They are many of them farmers, cultivating the lands surrounding the village. David keeps the store: the general produce of the community is deposited with him, and is conveyed to York, for sale, regularly twice a-week; and he accounts to the different members for the amount of produce sent to market. This David Wilson is a singular and original character: he is very anxious to obtain converts to his creed, for which purpose he goes about to the different villages, for twenty miles or more, to deliver his doctrines. He frequently preaches in York; and wherever he goes, he draws large congregations,—not only to hear his preaching, which is purely original, but also his singing men, his musicians, and his virgins,—some of which always follow in his train.

David, in person, is of the middle stature, about sixty years of age, a healthy looking man; he squints much, and has a flat heavy appearance. He, in common with the whole of the sect, wears a homespun blueish mixture: his walk is peculiar,—he appears to move as if he were pulling his legs after him; his speech has a strong nasal twang,—his dwelling is a large respectable house near the temple,—the virgins have a separate apartment,—they are all kept well employed; some at spinning, others sewing, and different kinds of work. The principle of the Davidites appears to be, a mutual assistance to each other. They are not absolutely embodied in one and the same society, as is the case with Mr. Owen's establishments: but though living in one community, and having their laws and regulations within themselves, yet, as to personal property, each individual is distinct. David obtained a large quantity of land, which he sells out to the different members of his sect. They all have separate farms, but each member turns in his surplus produce to David for advances, &c., made; they severally contribute towards the general expenses of the establishment,—such as building their temple, or any other undertaking for their general accommodation. Any man who has a farm or other occupation may, if he choose, become a convert to this sect, and join in the community,—submitting, of course, to their laws and regulations. This singular sect, though professing the doctrines of Christianity, appear to consider it as indispensable to unite with it as much as possible the observance of some part of the ordinances contained in the Mosaic law. They profess to take the model of their institution from some parts of the book of Kings.

David has an establishment of virgins, who keep up an annual feast, after the manner of the feast of Belshazzar, and some other religious observances, in accordance with the ancient Mosaic institutions. On the occasion of their annual feast, they prepare the most sumptuous and expensive entertainment, which is open to all who choose to attend. There is music, dancing, and every demonstration of joy. The Davidites, although strictly enforcing the rigid principles of their doctrine, do not conform themselves in the outward man, at least, as far as regards their dress, to any particular plainness of habit. The virgins, when seen at a place of worship, are all dressed in white, and uniformly. They, together with all the women belonging to the sect, used to be drilled to the use of fire-arms, probably in case of extremity, to defend themselves; on one occasion, however, one of their muskets burst, after which accident they declined the practice. Any of the unmarried men of the sect, who takes a fancy to either of the virgins, makes known his ideas to David, who communicates to her the proposal made; and if she should wish to enter into the holy state of matrimony, an appointment is made for a meeting of two hours' duration; (which is all that is allowed;) and when a final decision, either favorable or otherwise, is made.

The sect of Davidites have not been located here more than about fifteen or twenty years. They give ample proof of having rapidly increased in number and property, which clearly demonstrate that where a settlement is closely connected,—where they are concentrated as nearly as possible,—where there are every means of communication that can be desired,—and where, in fact, they study each others' interests,—it is then that settlements will prosper.

Each individual has his own immediate success at stake; which is a wholesome stimulus to every man's exertion; although the whole body have a corresponding feeling for the success and prosperity of each other; for they are well aware, that although each distinct member depends on himself, yet if the whole body be not prosperous, it must operate in some degree inimical to the interest of all.

The country around Newmarket is much settled by Quakers; particularly the township of Whitchurch. They are a most industrious class of people: those to be met with in many parts, are of peculiarly reserved, shy, primitive kind of habits, unsociable and apparently have little or no correspondence with the rest of mankind. But the Quakers, settled hereabouts, are of a very different character; for though they have a peculiarity of manners, yet they are a cheerful, free, pleasant people and extremely hospitable. They are branches of the original sect settled in Pennsylvania, and many of them are wealthy, and appear to live in very comfortable circumstances. Their houses are always open to strangers, and the best their house affords.

The road leading towards Lake Simcoe, through the township of Georgina, is well settled. Here is rather a large settlement of half-pay officers, who appear to live very respectably. Lake Simcoe is about twenty miles across, and is in the direct line with Penetanguishene. About seventy miles above Newmarket, Lake Simcoe is a beautiful picturesque spot, affording an abundance of fish, particularly salmon, which are taken here, both in winter and summer.

Penetanguishene is a station of the government, where a strong garrison is regularly kept up. As a point of defence, it is most judiciously chosen, and is capable of defending a large tract of country. It is so defended by nature, that no enemy could ever surprise it. This post is at the extremity of the settled part of Upper Canada. The climate here is much the same as in other parts of the Upper Province; probably the winters are a little shorter: but they are in some seasons very severe, —the thermometer frequently at twenty-five and thirty degrees below zero. This is a part of the globe where the Northern Lights, or the Aurora Borealis, are seen to great perfection. Sometimes they appear absolutely to blaze in the air.

The country further northward is very imperfectly, if at all known, except to the Indians; and they have a particular antipathy against giving any information whatever respecting the extreme inland parts of the country; they are afraid, as they say, of *White Man*, lest they should destroy their hunting ground.

The country between Lake Simcoe and Penetanguishene is but partially settled. The situation is as yet too insulated for settlers; the soil and climate are good; and in the course of a few more years, there is no doubt but this will become a flourishing part of the province.

The other main road out of York is called Dundas-street, which leads round by Hamilton to Niagara, a distance by land of one hundred miles. Niagara and the immediate surrounding country is now styled the garden of the Upper Province. Certain it is, that in the neighborhood of Niagara, Queenstown, St. Catharines, &c., the climate is peculiarly mild, and vegetation flourishes in an astonishing degree. Dundas-street was originally intended to extend from Kingston to Talbot's settlement, a distance of five hundred miles. The whole line of road is now laid out and traversed; but the only part of it that is known as Dundas-street, is that between York and Dundas, a distance of fifty miles. At the commencement of this road, out of York, during about seven miles, are the plains, or high lands; the country has then a more interesting appearance, and is remarkably well settled. About ten miles from York is an excellent inn, kept by a Yorkshireman,—a man whose whole attention and interest seem to be devoted to the health and well-being of his horses. This person keeps a good house, and is the chief proprietor of the stages running between York and Hamilton, for it is now a regular stage thoroughfare from York round to Niagara, and the road is excellent all the way. The road from York to

Hamilton is remarkable for the most picturesque scenery that is probably to be met with on any road of the same distance in the world: the deep glens give it a peculiar novelty. In some of these glens you have to descend a declivity of a mile or more, so perpendicular, that on the approach to it you appear to be going straight forward from the edge of one precipice to the other,—(for the valley is not a quarter of a mile wide at the bottom,)—when all at once the immense gulf beneath opens to the view;—particularly at what is called the Sixteen Mile Creek.

A few miles from this place, is the interesting Indian village, called Hurontario. It is composed of about forty houses, inhabited wholly by Indians. They have each a few acres of land attached to their dwellings, for the purpose of raising vegetables, &c. They follow their usual occupations of hunting, fishing, &c., and are by far the most civilized body of Indians that are to be met with in the Canadas. They are a remnant of the tribe of the late celebrated Indian Chief *Tecumseh*,—a Chief who distinguished himself in a very remarkable manner in the last American war in which he was slain.

Tecumseh was the *Napoleon* among the Indians of the West. He fought and led on his bands most heroically, in concert with the British troops, against the American forces, and fell nobly, and was deeply lamented. His name was equally a terror to his enemies, as it was eulogized and venerated by his immediate followers. Our government, as a reward for the merits of this tribe, has been at the entire expense of building this village for their removal. It also makes them annual presents of blankets, provisions, &c. There is a school established in the village, which is most ably conducted by a Mr. Jones, a native of the tribe, but who has received a good education in England, and is a well-informed, gentlemanly young man. They have a chapel, and Mr. Jones is also their minister. At their devotions they appear to be most devout and attentive. They have deposited with them an English standard, which they fail not to hoist on any particular occasion,—such as a visit from the governor, &c.

The village of Hurontario is the picture of neatness and cleanliness; and it imparts a most pleasant feeling to see these poor savages now reclaimed from a life of barbarism and ignorance, living in comfort and prosperity, and under the dictates of a pure and rational religion.

Dundas-street is so remarkably well settled,— there are so many good inns, excellent farm-houses surrounded by thriving young well-bearing orchards, the whole of the road interspersed with many handsome villas, some very superior,—that it naturally suggests to the mind of the traveller, of his passing through a country on the other side of the Atlantic.

About thirty miles above York was, some few years ago, the residence of Mr. Galt, the ex-superintendant of the Canada Company's affairs here. It is a most delightful spot, having a very extensive view both over a large tract of inland country, and also over Lake Ontario, Burlington Bay, &c. Here the road to Guelph branches off out of the Dundas-street. It is from hence twenty-six miles. This is the only place in Canada where hand-posts are put up to denote the places and distance to where the roads lead; probably these were erected by the Company. The road to Guelph is good, and pretty well settled. The city was laid out and built principally by the Canada Company: it bears the name in honor to the royal family of England. It is a scattered kind of place. There are a few tolerable good inns,—mechanics of various grades, smiths, carpenters, a grist and saw mill, a brewery, &c. This was intended as the principal station of the Company, and doubtless they anticipated a rapid flow of settlers to accumulate in its neighborhood, but this expectation has not been altogether realized; however, it must be recollected that Guelph is as yet quite in its infancy: five years ago, and the place was not. There are some settlers in its vicinity, who appear to be getting about them the comforts of life. They have many of them tolerable good clearances, plenty of stock, comfortable houses, &c., and seem to be well contented. It is astonishing with what patience and fortitude, many new settlers endure their first hardships, and in some cases they are of no ordinary stamp; yet it must be borne in mind, that they have the strongest and most rational stimulants to persevere and overcome present difficulties,—to forego, at least for a time, many of the comforts of life. They feel they are working on their *own* soil, their *freehold* land, and either he or his family will one day or other reap the advantages. These recollections seem to sweeten all the toils and fatigues endured more or less by every new settler. Every acre of land he converts from the wilderness into cultivation is his own; every tree he fells, adds to his real property. These are stimulants that will naturally operate on the mind of every man, to urge him on in spite of a little present fatigue and privation; to make every effort in his power to become the independent possessor of the soil he treads on, and that which will supply food for himself and family.

On the Dundas-street, about fifteen miles farther, is the little picturesque town of Dundas, situated at the bottom of an immensely deep glen; the road ascends for many miles before coming to this glen, it then descends at least three miles, and is in some places very steep, down to the town of Dundas. It is a little compact, neat place, of some business too. There are four or five stores of rather a superior kind. Dundas is a place that will immediately strike the traveller who has ever seen the romantic scenery of Switzerland. It is surrounded on every side by hills, rising abruptly above the town, which are traversed in every direction by circuitous winding paths leading to the numerous dwellings—built, some on the summit, and others on the sides of those hills. Dundas is a second Switzerland; its romantic scenery is worth travelling a long distance to see: it is a place of considerable trade with the more inland country, and likely to become more so. A canal, called Desjardins' Canal, is now nearly completed, to communicate between Dundas and Hamilton, a distance of five miles, where it unites with the navigation at the head of Lake Ontario. In this part of the country, there is quite an accumulation of small towns. There are Dundas, Ancaster, and Hamilton, all places of considerable business and population, and all within ten miles of each other. Ancaster is much larger than Dundas; it is a place of longer standing, and more business. There are no other parts of the province that bear comparison with this neighborhood; the roads, the buildings, the farms, and towns, are on a very superior scale; the inns particularly, are conducted in a much better style than those in many other parts of the province.

Ancaster is a prosperous bustling town; it has all the appearance of a regular established place; it resembles many others, when its prosperity is insured by the spirit and enterprise of its inhabitants. Such appears to be the character of the merchants of Ancaster; they show all the characteristics of bustling activity; they are shop-keepers, merchants, farmers, potash-makers, bankers—in fact, they unite all the chief services of the prosperity of the country within themselves.

Ancaster lies in the direct road to the now attractive settlement of London, in the western district. This settlement is about eighty miles above Ancaster; the roads all the way are good. The London settlement is now becoming a place of as much attraction as any new place in the province.

It is situated on the river Thames, flowing into Lake Erie. There are the towns of London, Westminster, Brentford, Richmond, Oxford, and many other familiar names, all newly sprung up here, and mostly on the river Thames. The lands in this part of the province are without doubt the most productive of any in the country. On new land, they frequently get here from fifty to sixty bushels of wheat to an acre. If they can average forty, or even thirty, at the price that wheat has been lately realizing, even in the remotest parts of the Upper Province, it must pay well. They have been getting, during the whole of this last season, a dollar a bushel. Now supposing a man buys a lot of land at four dollars an acre, which is the highest price for wild land, unless in peculiar situations, (be it observed here, that all purchasers of land in this country ought to calculate, that out of every hundred acres he buys, he must expect, upon an average, to get twenty acres of uncultivatable land,) consequently it will cost him twenty-five shillings an acre, the cost of twenty acres, therefore, would be twenty-five pounds; to chop it will be about eight dollars an acre, forty pounds; to log, burn, and fence it, about eight dollars an acre more, another forty pounds; the seed necessary for twenty acres, will be twenty bushels—

twenty dollars, or five pounds; a bushel of wheat to an acre is quite enough for new land; if more is sown it is worse than a loss of seed; for it tends to stifle the growth of the whole; the cutting, housing, and threshing of the above crop would be about twenty pounds more, making a total outlay of one hundred and thirty pounds. Now supposing the land to average a crop of thirty bushels to the acre, which would be six hundred bushels, at a dollar a bushel—six hundred dollars—one hundred and fifty pounds being a surplus of twenty pounds over the whole outlay; thus the first crop would pay for the land, clearing it, and putting it in a state of cultivation. The calculation here made, is upon the consideration that the settler hires and pays for all the labor necessary to complete the above undertaking. But suppose him to be an industrious character, working hard himself, or having a large family, with sons able to assist him, by which means he might be able to do all, or nearly all within himself. What an important saving this would be! and people with large families, if well brought up, have a much better chance of succeeding here than those without.

The settlement of London is rapidly accumulating, and there is little doubt that this will be one of the finest parts of Upper Canada, when the means of transport for their surplus produce are better established, such as the Welland and Rideau Canals, &c. There are many persons from the older settlements flocking to this new place of attraction. London and Westminster are but yet very small and thinly populated places, but in the country between them are many good farms, while the lands are being fast taken up, and the trees are rapidly cut. Oxford is already a pretty little village, containing some twenty or thirty houses, and is one of those new interesting little villages just budding into existence. The remarkable goodness of the roads here, as well as the fertility of the soil, will greatly tend to the increase of these new settlements. The climate, likewise, is more temperate than in the northern parts of the province. Fruit of all descriptions grow in prodigious quantities, and peaches, in particular, are plentiful enough to feed pigs on, and they form a very good and fattening food. The forest in this part has altogether a different appearance to what it presents in any other part of the province. There is little or no underbrush. The trees are so wide apart in some places, that a coach and six might be drawn amongst them, and the timber very large and tall, a circumstance that denotes, amongst other criterions, the richness and goodness of the soil. This is a part of the country where the wild turkeys will occasionally be met with; they are sometimes in flocks of twenty and thirty together; they are larger than the tame turkeys, sometimes weighing thirty-seven pounds; they run exceedingly fast, and, in fact, seldom attempt to fly, trusting to the swiftness of their speed in running as their means of escape, resembling, in this respect, the ostrich.

Beyond the London settlement, on the shores of Lake Erie, is the celebrated and extensive settlement of Colonel Talbot, known as Talbot's Settlement, extending many miles. Colonel Talbot, the original settler, obtained from government a very extensive grant of lands, upon the condition of his making actual settlements on it, and from every settler whom he can induce to locate on a lot of land, he has the privilege of retaining a certain other portion. The Colonel has been here many years, has a very large farm and establishment, and under his management the settlement has increased prodigiously. It is the extent of the province in this direction, being on the borders of Lake Erie, which divides Canada from the United States.

Hamilton, situated at the very head of the Lake Ontario, is about ten miles below Ancaster, at the head of Lake Ontario; it is a place that has grown up entirely within these few years, as about five years ago, not a vestige of it was in existence; it now contains a population of fifteen hundred or two thousand inhabitants. Lake Ontario is rather of a triangular shape, about two hundred miles in length, and averaging about eighty to one hundred miles in breadth, taking the distance from Prescott to York. The part between York and Niagara might be taken as absolutely the extent of the lake itself, but at this portion commences an inlet of the lake, which runs up fifty miles, at the head of which inlet the town of Hamilton is built.

The accumulated waters of this country, flowing into a comparatively small channel, forms a matter of deep consideration for the contemplative mind; here are the waters of Ontario, the least of the three sisters; Erie next, and Huron a giantess to either of them; and all these inland seas pour their united torrents into the noble St. Lawrence. In addition to these, are the waters of the Ottawa, with her thousand streams forming their junction in a manner truly astonishing; the wonder naturally created in the mind is, how these accumulated bodies can find vent in a stream so comparatively small; yet such is the fact. Neither Huron,

K

Erie nor Ontario, has any other outlet, and Ottawa flows immediately into Lake St. Louis, and there joins the St. Lawrence; nor is the St. Lawrence of that depth, to account satisfactorily for the accumulation of so vast a body.

The extent of the vast inland resources of navigation of this country, can be estimated only in a very minor degree by the appearance even of the St. Lawrence; when the means now in operation are completed, there will be a route of unbroken inland navigation for a distance of from seven hundred to a thousand miles, taking the route from Lachine, by the Ottawa, to Grenville, through its canal again into the Ottawa to the mouth of the Rideau Canal, and by it to Kingston, from thence by Lake Ontario to the Welland Canal, and through which, into Lake Erie. These great water communications offer the means of an inland navigation, of an extent probably, unparalleled in the world. What an amazing extent of country is here, nine tenths and more of which, are yet in a useless state! What if we have forty thousand emigrants out this season, scatter them over these provinces, and where are they felt? It is true, that they may at first rush in like a torrent, and stop up the passages leading to the regular and natural channels of their several destinations, but let them spread themselves regularly and gradually over the country, let them go where their assistance is really wanted, and it will be found that an annual addition of emigrants, almost to any amount, is what these provinces will still stand in need of for many years to come.

Hamilton, mentioned before, at the head of Ontario, and immediately communicating with its waters, is the place where all the produce coming from Dundas, Ancaster, and the places above, is shipped for transportation downward. When the canal (Desjardins) which is to communicate with Dundas, &c., is finished, Hamilton must become a place of considerable importance; it is already a bustling, busy town, increasing fast in population, buildings, and trade, and is a great thoroughfare both in summer and winter; in the former season a steamer comes up from York, and another daily from Niagara, it lies also in the immediate route, by land, between York and Niagara, and also takes in the thoroughfare from the London District, the settlements on the shores of Lake Erie, &c.; in fact, Hamilton is one of those new places just dawning into prosperity; not that these symptoms of the rising importance of the country are confined to Hamilton or to any other given place, they are general and observable in every part of Canada, and while she enjoys the present liberal policy of her mother country, she must go on and prosper in her commerce and agriculture.

A little below Hamilton is Burlington Bay, formed in a singular manner by a narrow shoal running across the inlet, about four miles broad; it is canaled in one part for the passage of vessels. Hamilton is situated exceedingly low, being surrounded by high lands on all sides, yet it appears not to be an unhealthy place, although, in hot weather, immense vapors arise here, but they ascend, and consequently, those residing in the lowest situations feel the least effect from them. A few years ago, the fever and ague was very prevalent, and it was remarked that those who resided in the most elevated situations, had it the most severely, indeed, the same remarks have applied to many other places. These diseases, however, are purely local, and they recede as the country becomes cleared and open; in fact, in the forest the natural climate of the country has not a fair chance; there is but little admission either of air or sun, from the thick foliage of the almost impervious forest, all is stagnant and humid; but clear away those impediments, open the country, admit a free current of air and the influence of the sun, and there will not be found a healthier climate in the world.

The tour of inhabited Canada is now very nearly made, but the most interesting wonder of the country, and that which is equally the astonishment and wonder of the world, remains yet to be seen, and such is the intense interest excited by this stupendous work of nature, that a person who has seen them ninety and nine times, would be equally anxious to view them the hundredth.

The FALLS OF NIAGARA are about sixty miles from Hamilton, the road from that place to the town of Niagara being fifty miles, and almost all by the lake shores. The first place of any consequence, after leaving Hamilton, is the pretty little town of St. Catharine, situated in the centre of a finely settled and cleared country; it contains about a thousand inhabitants, the houses and buildings are exceedingly good, and its site is on a rising ground, which keeps the place at all times dry and clean. The face of the surrounding country assumes quite a different appearance to that apparent in many other parts of Canada. The forest can be seen only at intervals, here is a continuation of farms upon rather a large scale, extensive tracts of cleared country, hill and dale, all open to view, with the comfortable looking farmhouse, snug and compact outbuildings, regularly square laid out fields, all well fenced, and none of those common excrescences of the country, the stumps.

The town of Niagara is situated at the mouth of the Niagara River, on the shores of Lake Ontario, eighteen miles below the falls, and is the largest and best town on the western side of the lake. This part of the country is called the Garden of Upper Canada, and certain it is, that the climate here, though only thirty-six miles across the lake from York, is much milder. Grapes grow here to a large size, also cherries, and in fact, all descriptions of fruit in prodigious quantities, and vegetables are raised nearly a month earlier than at York. Niagara is not by any means a place of the commercial importance of York, nor has it the numerous settled townships presented in the vicinity of that place, it will be observed, that this is the extent of the British territories in Upper Canada, consequently, it has not the number of back settlements to support its trade as is the case with its sister town, still Niagara is considered of sufficient importance to send a representative to the house of assembly. Niagara is not considered so healthy a situation as some other parts of the province, being very subject to the lake fever, certain it is, that the inhabitants generally, have not so healthy an appearance, they have a yellowish kind of color, and are termed the yellow heads; the town is a very great thoroughfare in the summer, it lies in the immediate way from York to the States, and to the falls; and the immense numbers of visiters flocking to and from the falls, in the course of the season, is a matter of no small consideration to the town, and renders it very animated and gay; numerous parties of pleasure from the States make this their regular tour in the summer; from hence to York, down the Ontario to Montreal, Quebec, &c.

Seven miles above Niagara, on the immediate banks of the river, is Queenston, a neat place, standing on very high ground, the banks of the river are here exceedingly steep and high, the river is about a quarter of a mile wide and very rapid. Queenston was the scene of many a sanguinary conflict during the last war, between the British and American forces, it was here that the lamented and brave General Brock, the hero of Upper Canada lost his life, he fell while gallantly leading his troops. This place immediately fronts Lewiston, the American frontier town on the opposite bank of the river Niagara. Lewiston is a handsome town, which appears to be newly built, it is already a place of some consequence; there are stages running daily from hence to Buffalo, Rochester, Lockport, Albany, New-York, &c. &c.

Queenston is eleven miles from the falls, and if the weather be still and calm a rumbling noise may be heard, it increases more and more, now producing the noise of distant thunder, still louder and louder, till at last it becomes a terrific roar: nothing can yet be seen of the falls, the river is rapid and its banks are very steep, the mind of the traveller is prepared for something extraordinary, every moment the long anticipated delight is expected, but when it bursts on the view, no pen can describe the sensations of amazement that are excited by first beholding those wondrous objects of sublimity and grandeur, the mind becomes lost in the mazes of its own reflections.

> Hark! on the winds, methinks I hear the roar
> Of "Waters—'tis a voice from that dark gulf"
> Where Erie meets Ontario—and it comes
> Like the deep yell of many wandering spirits.
> Niagara! who that has ever seen
> Thy torrents of a thousand streams and lakes,
> Their dark deep foaming mass of waters pour
> Into thy foaming chasm of death, or gaz'd
> As it did rush, as 'twere, from the infinite height
> Of Heaven, and seem'd as it had hence brought down
> The rainbow, blast, and thunder, such the light
> Around thy brow, and sudden rush of winds—
> And ceaseless, ponderous peals of sound,—or who
> Hath been beneath these everlasting walls
> Of tumbling torrent, and unshaken rock,

Arch'd as a palace of magnificence,
Where nature reigns in dark sublimity,
And felt not an oppressive sense of power
And majesty of Him, who thus doth pour
The cataract from his palm.
  Niagara! if now thou'rt grand—
Far grander still, when haunts of men were not
Upon thy shore, and the vast solitude
Of boundless, trackless wilderness, through which
Thou'st worn thy deep and rock-bound path, appeared,
Awe struck, to tremble at thy dreadful voice.

About five miles above the cataract, the river expands to the dimensions of a lake, after which it gradually narrows; the rapids commence at the upper extremity of Goat Island, which is half a mile in length, and divides the river at the point of precipitation into two unequal parts, the largest is distinguished by the several names of Horseshoe, Crescent and British Fall, from its semicircular form and contiguity to the Canadian shore; the smaller is named the American Fall, which is divided by a rock from Goat Island. The current runs about six miles an hour, but supposing it to be only five, the quantity of water which passes the falls in an hour is more than 85,000,000 of tons avoirdupois; if we suppose it to be six, it will be more than 102,000,000, and in a day would exceed 24,000,000,000 of tons.

On visiting the cavern beneath the fall, the traveller should take advantage of a fine morning, and after providing himself with a guide, set out as early as six o'clock, that he might have the advantage of the sun upon the waters, he should disencumber himself of such garments as he does not care to have wetted; descending the circular ladder, he follows the course of the path running along the top of the *debris* of the precipice, and having pursued this tract for about eighty yards, in the course of which he will get completely drenched, he finds himself close to the cataract, although enveloped in a cloud of spray, the direction of the path and the nature of the cavern about to be entered may be readily distinguished: the difficulty in respiration is very great when surrounded by the spray, and after being blown about, and buffetted by the wind, stunned by the noise, and blinded by the spray, (each successive gust penetrating the very bones with cold,) he at length arrives, and having collected his senses by degrees, the wonders of this cavern slowly develope themselves; it is impossible to describe the strange unnatural light reflecting through its crystal walls, the roar of the waters and the blasts of the hurricane, which perpetually rages in its recesses. The cavern is tolerably light, and the sun may clearly be distinguished through the watery barrier; the fall of the cataract is nearly perpendicular, the bank over which it is precipitated is of a concave form, owing to its upper stratum being composed of limestone, and its base of soft slabstone, which has been eaten away by the constant attrition of the recoiling waters. The cavern is about one hundred and twenty feet in height, fifty in breadth, and three hundred in length. There is one other point which may be visited, except the wind blow full upon the sheet of the cataract, when it drives the water with great force against a point of the rock which must be passed, and thus cuts off the communication: a few yards beyond, the precipice becomes perpendicular and blends with the water, forming the extremity of the cave; the eel and the water-snake crawl about its recesses in considerable numbers.

In September, 1827, a very singular and interesting spectacle, of which due notice had been given for months before, took place at the Falls of Niagara; from ten to twelve thousand persons from all parts of the Canadas and the United States were present. There are three good and extensive hotels near the falls, and the proprietors, with the view of attracting the attention of the company, purchased an old sloop, called the Michigan, which had been a lake vessel for some years, of about four hundred tons burden, to descend, or rather to be hurled, over the falls. The extreme novelty of the sight, had attracted immense bodies of people, and what added highly to the curiosity was, that her crew consisted of wild animals; there were shipped on board, a few miles above the falls, two huge bears, two wolves, some racoons, foxes, deer, pigs, geese, &c. &c. She was towed down the lake, very near the falls, by the Queenston steam-boat; when the Michigan got near to the precipice, she went over on one side, of which accident, the bears, more on the alert than their brother shipmates, took prompt advantage, for they no sooner found the vessel stranded, than they made a plunge in the water and swam safely to the shore, to the no small diversion of the bystanders; the vessel, however, soon righted and came over the precipice (a fall of one hundred and sixty feet) with a most tremendous crash—she broke right in two, and the only living animal taken out of her was one of the geese.

There is an idea entertained, and by no means an unfeasible one, that the falls at one time were much farther down the river towards Ontario, or even quite near the lake itself, this is by no means improbable, for the perpetual attrition of the waters, on a substance however hard it may be, must in the space of time considerably wear it away; a gentleman, who lives close by the falls, has observed, that within the period of his residence here, they have visibly receded.

The great accumulation of visitors to the falls, in the course of a season, affords a rich harvest to the hotel keepers and others who live in their immediate vicinity, and they are always on the alert to devise some novel and extraordinary feat, independant of the natural attractiveness of the place. To amuse and prolong the stay of visitors, for some seasons past, they have had an annual fall jumper, in the person of *Sam Patch*, who has since at one fell swoop, jumped into another world; this Sam Patch made the leap of Niagara Falls more than once with safety, he jumped from the top of the precipice of the highest fall, into the gulf below, an undertaking of unparalleled boldness. The tremendous rushing of the waters into the cauldron below, the perpetual foaming and roaring of the troubled element, the immense height of the torrent, and all the features of this vast scene, are quite enough to appal the mind of any beholder; but for a man to hurl himself from the top, and plunge into the foaming waters below, shows a daring of no ordinary stamp; however, this man performed it with safety, he came out quite unhurt at a short distance below the falls. At another place he repeated this feat once too often; he was hired to jump the Genesee Falls some miles below Rochester, in the States: the Genesee Falls are small when compared with those of Niagara, and in order still to increase the novelty of the scene, a stage was erected at the top of the fall, so as to elevate the height of the jump that this unfortunate man was to make, it is said that he was somewhat in liquor at the time, he flung himself off and never was seen alive again; he was taken out of the water a few miles below the falls quite dead; it was said he lost his usual confidence at this last attempt.

Birds.—The feathered tribes of Canada are extremely numerous; many of the kinds are to be seen only at stated times of the year; indeed there are many different species, known only to those who happen to go into the peculiar parts of the country which they inhabit; and, as has been before observed, no kind of birds, and scarcely any living wild animal, is to be seen here in the dead of winter; in fact, the natural productions of this country are only to be known by a residence of some years, and it is only by penetrating the forest, and closely observing its almost hidden productions, that any just idea can be formed of its natural capabilities.

The Canadian Partridge or Pheasant, is nearly

as large as the European Hen Pheasant, of much the same color, and spotted on the breast; but the most remarkable feature in the Canadian Partridge is its tail, which is, when spread, the shape and size of a fan, it has decidedly more the habits of the pheasant than of the partridge, it pitches in the trees, and has the same motion when on the ground, with many other habits peculiar to the pheasant at home, its flesh too is very similar in flavor and delicacy of appearance; the hen lays fourteen or sixteen eggs; they have a very singular habit, in the laying season, which is termed drumming, it is the cock bird calling his mate; this he does by perching on a log of wood or a stump, and about every ten minutes, through the day, he makes a buzzing kind of noise by fluttering his wings and feathers for a few minutes, and ends by flapping his wings hard against his sides in repeated strokes, which at a little distance has very much the sound of a muffled drum; this habit often proves fatal to them, for they are easily discovered by this noise, and although it is at a time of the year when they ought not to be killed, the settler does not often scruple to do so, being seldom guided by true sportsmanlike principles; the Canadian Partridge is at all times a stupid bird, and a person may approach very near to them.

They sometimes flock together in coveys, but in general are to be seen only by two or three together. It is a singular fact, that should there be a dozen or more of these birds on a tree, the sportsman may keep firing, provided he take the lowest bird first at each shot, and insure himself the whole covey, but he must not stop to pick them up, but keep on firing till they are all killed; by taking the under bird at each shot, so that it does not fall to disturb any of the others, and keeping up the noise by firing or whistling, he attracts their attention and keeps them from flying away.

The bird that most resembles the European Partridge in all but in disparity of size, is called here the quail; they are precisely the same in form and color, and have all the habits peculiar to those birds; they keep together in coveys of considerable numbers; they are to be met with in the field after the grain is taken away; they never pitch in bushes or trees; they fly low, have the same creeping manner of moving, and are in every respect the same kind of bird; they are very fat and delicious eating, but are rarely if ever seen in the northern parts of Canada; they are very numerous near and above York, and in the upper districts. There is to be seen occasionally, in the winter, near the Ottawa, the White Partridge, the partridge inhabiting any part of Upper Canada, as high as fifty miles above the Chats, do *not* turn white, as has been stated by some writers, they retain their brown color all the winter; those which are seen about that neighborhood are migraters from the north west.

There are two kinds of plovers, the gray and the black and white, the gray plover is mostly to be seen in the fall of the year; they are a very shy bird, fat and good eating; the black and white plover, though very rarely seen in northern Canada, are to be met with in immense flocks above York, and in the western districts, so much so as sometimes to darken the air; they are much larger than the gray plover: the plover, like the pigeon, is not a native of Canada, but migrates from the south; they are met at some periods of the year crossing and recrossing the lakes in the upper country, thus they must fly some hundreds of miles at a stretch. Woodcocks are plenty in the low marshy parts of the country, they are not more than two thirds the size of the English Woodcock, but are much the same in color and richness of flavor. The Canadian Snipe is very nearly the same as that of Europe.

There are four kinds of woodpeckers in Canada, the black, the brown and red, or pigeon woodpecker, the white and red, and the small speckled; the black woodpecker, or cock of the woods, as he is generally called, is something larger than a pigeon, and is a handsome bird; the body is black; under the wings yellow and white; a bright crimson tuft on the cap of its head, with a white ring round the eyes; it has a remarkably strong, clear and shrill note, and is a prognosticator of the weather, for it is generally remarked, that when it is more vociferous than usual, it portends rain; it has an amazingly strong beak, and a tongue that will extend nearly a foot in length, the end of which is tipped with a hard bony substance, and bores the same as a gimblet; this bird keeps mostly in the woods. Woodpeckers in general, are great forewarners of danger, for they leave those unequivocal marks in all the rotten and decayed trees, by which means they are easily discovered in the forests.

The brown or pigeon woodpecker, is about the same size as a pigeon; this is also a handsome bird; it is of a bright yellowish brown, speckled on the breast; a tuft of gold color on its back, with a red poll. This bird mostly frequents the open clearances, and is sometimes seen in flocks together. They are good eating.

The small speckled woodpecker appears to be a solitary bird, seldom seen in company, and inhabiting the secluded part of the woods; it is small, but appears to possess prodigious strength in its head and neck.

The white and red, or quarrelsome woodpecker, is always to be found in the clearances and about the buildings; they are eternally quarrelling and fighting with each other, which sometimes even ends in the death of one of them. They are rather a small bird, white on the back, with black breasts and wings, and red heads; the noise which these birds make in boring with their beaks, is beyond conception; they do great mischief in shingled roof houses, which they bore to get at the grubs, &c., and which sounds, to a person in the inside, the same as the boring of an auger.

Some of the birds of this country, are of extreme richness and brilliancy of plumage, the most conspicuous of which is the cardinal. The cardinal is a bird only to be seen in the extreme western parts of the upper province, and then but rarely; it is more common in the States; the cardinal is so named from its having, longitudinally, streaks on its body, of scarlet and black, somewhat similar to the splendid robes worn by those high dignitaries; it is about the size of the blackbird; the colors of its plumage are inconceivably

L

bright, and it has an appearance, when flying, of dazzling splendor.

The fire bird is of a deep red colour, with a little black on its head and wings; it is about the size of the lark, and is to be seen in most parts of the province.

The Canadian King-fisher is about the same size as the European, very much inferior with regard to brilliancy of plumage, being rather an ugly bird, but precisely the same in its habits.

The Loon is a singular bird, it inhabits the water, is never seen out of it, and is therefore never seen to fly; it is nearly as large as the goose, and has a black head, with a white ring round its neck, and speckled body; its skin is so thick, tough and strong, that bags are made of it for the preservation of any thing from wet; the Loon is continually diving in the water after the fish; it is extremely difficult to kill.

Of all the singular and interesting little members of the feathered community, the Humming Bird stands the foremost; it is a native of the States, but migrates in the summer, and is occasionally seen in all parts of the Canadas; they are of different colors and sizes; some are not much larger than a cock-chafer; their color can scarcely be

CANADA AS IT IS.

descried until they are caught, for they are in an incessant buz and flutter; they appear seldom to alight on any thing, but in their continual fluttering, they dip their little beaks first in one flower and then in another; they seem to live entirely by the suction they derive from different flowers, particularly from the blossom of *scarlet beans;* they are of a variety of colors, green, blue, yellow, purple, &c., the only way to shoot them is to load a gun with sand instead of shot. Under no circumstances can the humming bird be tamed, or bear the least confinement.

There are two kinds of owls in Canada; they are both large, the smallest kind is larger than the common owl at home; they make a most horrible screeching noise in the night, and in the forests it is heard for miles when the weather is calm; the largest kind is the horned owl, which is an immense bird, much larger in body than the turkey; this owl, with its pointed horns and immense glaring eyes, has a most terrific appearance, particularly when come upon suddenly in the woods, for they generally appear sleeping; and when first disturbed, they look as if they would at once devour you; these birds are fortunately not very numerous; they sometimes do much mischief by devouring fowls, geese, turkeys, and even young

**IMAGE EVALUATION
TEST TARGET (MT-3)**

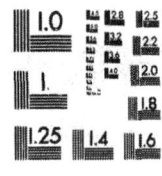

Photographic
Sciences
Corporation

23 WEST MAIN STREET
WEBSTER, N.Y. 14580
(716) 872-4503

pigs; they have in many respects more of the ferocity and habits of the hawk.

Of hawks there are four kinds, the largest is the hen hawk, which is very large, and will be often seen hovering around the houses and barns, and if an opportunity offer it will dart down and take up a hen or a chicken, or indeed both in his talons, and fly off with them; the next in size is the fishing hawk, this bird is a most expert fisherman, it sits watching on the brink of the stream, and the instant a fish appears, it dives into the water, and seldom fails in obtaining its prey; it is a singular sight to see them flying through the air, with probably a large pike or other fish securely locked in their talons; the sparrow hawk is of the smallest description, its prey is on small birds; the night hawk is a curious bird, appearing only at night; it ascends through the night with rapid flight to an immense height, and then suddenly drops itself to the ground as if shot; this is probably some manœuvre to catch the numerous flies that hover in the air by night.

There is in Canada a pretty singing bird called Tom-o-lincoln, it is about the size of the black-bird, it is generally to be seen in meadows, perched in small bushes, and sings most melodiously and in great variety of notes.

The Canadian Nightingale is the evening songster of the forest; as the sun is taking his final leave, the chaste notes of the nightingale are heard thrilling through the deep recesses of the woods; there is a peculiar plaintiveness in them, yet sweet and melodious in their effect.

The Thrush is a bird much the same in size as the English Thrush, but different in colour, it is of a dingy yellow, with a very long tail; it sings harmoniously, and in other respects precisely the same as that of Europe.

In the fall of the year starlings are observed in large flocks, to proclaim the approach of winter.

The Canadian Black-bird is generally to be found in marshy places; it is about the size of the thrush, of a glossy black colour, having some red on the tip of its wings.

Snow bird: this is a bird that is never seen but when the snow is on the ground; it is much about the size of the lark, with a considerable portion of white in its color: they fly in very large flocks.

The Canadian Lark is in size much the same as the English Sky Lark, but it keeps entirely on the ground.

The goldfinch or canary is more in colour like the latter, being of a bright yellow, or gold color, intermixed with a little black; it appears to be of the same habits as the goldfinch at home.

Of sparrows there are three kinds, which appear to have much the same habits as sparrows in general, but widely different in color; the first and largest is a bird not generally seen till the fall; it is of a bright azure color and looks very pretty; the next is smaller, and of a deep blue color; the other kind is still smaller, and of a perfect green color; so totally unlike any other small birds, which are generally of a brownish hue; these little bright plumaged birds have a very pretty appearance.

The largest of the feathered tribe here, is the bald-headed eagle; this is a very sagacious bird, very powerful and rarely to be approached; the bald-head is easily to be distinguished in its lofty flight. One of these birds was shot in the upper country some time ago, which measured from the tip of one wing to that of the other, thirteen feet, and from the point of the beak to the end of its tail, five feet ten inches; they mostly inhabit the tops of the mountains, or any other unfrequented spots.

Here are four kinds of wild ducks, the black, the red head, the wood duck, and the common brown water duck. The black duck is a very fine bird; in size between the tame duck and goose; its flesh is rich and good; the red heads are nearly as large as the black duck, and are also a very excellent eating bird; the wood duck is of a light brown color, unlike any other of its species; it pitches in the trees, and builds its nests there also; the common dark brown water duck is of the usual size; all these species are to be met with more or less through the provinces, but in the upper country, in the fall of the year, they flock together in myriads on the lakes.

Of tame fowl there is an abundance kept in both provinces, with the exception of ducks, and these are generally very scarce throughout the country.

Of tame geese there is an abundance all over the country, and they are profitable from the quantity of feathers they produce; it is the custom here, to pluck them alive once or twice a-year, and thus procure vast quantities of feathers; they are here yoked in the same manner as pigs, to prevent them getting into the grain, &c., which presents rather a curious appearance.

The upper country is an excellent climate for turkeys, of which there are in many places vast numbers bred. The common fowls too, thrive exceedingly well here. There are, in addition to the kinds described above, a great variety of water fowl, widgeon, teal, &c. &c.

The Canadian Rabbit or Hare, is in size between the two, but nearer to the latter, and has also more of its habits, than of the former; it does not burrow in the earth; in color too, it resembles the European Hare, or at least in summer; in the winter this animal turns nearly white; when the snow is on the ground, they will run to and fro on the same tracts for nights together, and are frequently taken by snaring.

The racoon is a short legged animal, with a thick body, long bushy tail, and a remarkably sharp pointed nose; it has a fair skin; when fat, they weigh from seven to ten pounds, their flesh is excellent eating.

Muskrat; this little animal, in its habits, much resembles the beaver, living in little houses curiously erected by the water side, so that they can approach their dwellings and emerge from them without being seen; it is in size scarcely as large as a cat; of a darkish brown color; they keep entirely in the water, except mornings and evenings; they are a disgusting looking animal; their flesh is eatable; but their fur is the most valuable part of them, and for which they are taken.

The martin is a kind of wild cat, it much resembles that domestic animal, but is not so large; it has a long slender body, small sharp head, and bushy tail; its fur is very fine, which is the object in hunting them; the fur of the martin, as well as that of the beaver, is an object of very considerable commerce.

There are two kinds of foxes in Canada, the black and the common red fox; the black fox is very rarely seen; its skin is very valuable; the common red fox is very frequent, and is a sly thief amongst the poultry, &c., their skins are of very little value; and such is the nature of the country yet, that they cannot be hunted with dogs with much success, though at Montreal some gentlemen have established a fox-hunting club; they turn out a large field of sportmen well mounted, with scarlet coats, caps quite in the regular jockey style, keep an excellent pack of hounds, and often get a fine run.

Squirrels, these little animals some seasons commit serious damage throughout the country; there are two kinds, the black and the red; the black are never in any numbers; they are a handsome little animal; the red squirrel is smaller than the English Squirrel, and not so handsome; these are the destructive kind, but they are not stationary; probably once in six or seven years they come in shoals, and destroy great quantities of grain; in 1827, they were here in myriads, when they did serious damage; many instances are known of their having cleared nearly whole fields of corn; and in one particular instance, they attacked a field of corn, and did not leave a single ear, it in fact almost ruined the poor settler; when they are in shoals, in this manner, it is almost impossible to keep them out of the corn; they travel through the country in regular droves, and swim the large rivers and lakes in large companies, journeying even thousands of miles.

The Canadian Porcupine is not so large as the African, but precisely the same in every other respect; it shoots its quills with considerable force when attacked; its flesh is excellent; the Indians appropriate the quills to many purposes of fanciful decorations.

The hedgehog, like that of Europe, has the same peculiar habit of rolling itself up like a ball, its prickles pointing outwards, forming a barrier against all attacks.

Ground hog: this little animal burrows in the ground like the rabbit, and has a head much like it, but with no other resemblance to that animal; it has a very thick body, remarkably short legs, so that it can run but slowly, and when seen above ground is easily taken; its flesh is good.

Skunk: this is an animal of much the same habits

as the polecat, but much larger; it is destructive to poultry; its chief means of defence appears to be carried in a small bag contained under its belly, and when attacked, it forces its contents at its assailant, the stink of which is so disgustingly offensive as to be almost insufferable.

Chip Monk: this little creature might be termed the rat of the country, it is a little thief of the most daring habits; it has not in color or make the least resemblance to the common rat, but its propensities are much the same; it is about as long as a guinea pig; and has a head much like that animal, but its body is not half so thick; the chip monk is continually to be seen about buildings and clearances; it is a provident little animal, taking care to lay in a good winter's store; its winter habitation is generally in the body of a hollow tree; on the approach of winter it very busily employs itself in securing grain or any other provisions within its reach, and this it does in a very singular manner, which is by cramming both sides of its cheeks with grain, or any thing else it can purloin, till they are ready to burst, and when met thus laden, they have a curious appearance.

Rats are not yet general in the province, but it is much to be feared that they will soon become so, for they are already at many places where the navigation touches at, conveyed by the steam-boats to different places. Both house and field mice are in abundance through the country.

The panther or American tiger, as it is sometimes called, is an inhabitant of Canada as well as of other parts [of the American continent; they are very rarely to be seen; they are neither so large, nor to be compared in beauty with the Bengal Tiger. Like other ravenous beasts of the forest, they prey upon the smaller animals, and when seen here, it is generally in chace of the racoon, of the flesh of which they seem particularly fond.

In treating of the reptiles of this country, there are not, as has been observed in a former part of this work, any venomous snakes in any part of the Canadas, lower than the head of Lake Ontario; there, in all the country above it, on the other side of the lake, about Niagara and the country extending to Lake Erie, as well as in almost every other part of the American continent, the rattlesnake is an inhabitant; the bite of this snake, though in some instances fatal, is not universally so; if proper remedies be applied at the instant of the accident, it is often cured; but this, though very venomous, is not the most dangerous snake on the American continent; there are two other kinds, each of which is more to be feared than the rattlesnake; these are the black snake, called the black chasir of Ohio, and the copper-headed snake, a very powerful creature, also an inhabitant of the States; the rattlesnake does not molest, even when approached, unless irritated, yet they do not fly from man as some other of the species, but lie and watch you as a cat; the copper-head, if approached, will immediately attack, and this they do in the most impetuous manner, they erect their heads, which they swell out to the size of a middling pig's head, and make a tremendous hissing noise, and wo be to those whom they may wound when in this state; the black chasir will follow and attack, and are the most dangerous reptile known. The rattlesnake and the copper-head are not at enmity with each other; on the contrary, they frequently cohabit together, an instance of which is the following: some two or three years ago, the inhabitants in the neighborhood of a place called Hillsborough, in Ohio, one of the western states of America, were so much annoyed with venomous snakes in their vicinity, that they were absolutely afraid to venture out of their houses. One of the inhabitants happened to discover a den of these snakes, that is, large holes in the rocks, where they were seen to creep in and out; the neighbors all agreed to make a "*snake destroying bee*," for this purpose they prepared themselves with long hooks, and took care duly to protect their persons; and in two days they hooked out of the crevices of the rock, upwards of two hundred snakes, mostly of the largest size, two thirds of which were rattlesnakes and the rest copper-heads, some of them measuring upwards of seven feet in length; the rattlesnake and the black chasir are mortal enemies, and when coming in close contact, one of them dies, generally the former; a battle was witnessed between these two dangerous reptiles in a secluded part of the country, in the western states, the attack was commenced by the black snake, and met by the rattlesnake with much ferocity, till disabled by the repeated bites of his antagonist; and, when lying prostrate, the black snake repeatedly bit his vanquished enemy until satisfied he was quite dead. The flesh of the rattlesnake is said to be good. In the digging of the Welland Canal, between Lakes Erie and Ontario, a few years ago, the workmen had occasion to blast a rock, in doing which, they met with a nest of rattlesnakes, there were sixty-four in number; in their rage, in being thus disturbed, some of them coiled themselves up, and bit their own bodies, and soon after swelled much, and died apparently in the greatest agony; but those that did not inflict the deadly wound on themselves, (after cutting off their heads, which contains the poison,) were cooked and eaten, and were said to be excellent. It is a singular fact, that the rattlesnake has an instinctive dread of the pig, which is exceedingly fond of the flesh of this snake; whenever people are annoyed by these reptiles near their dwellings, they have only to keep a number of pigs, and they are sure to get rid of them; the rattlesnake will bite the horse and the cow, and many instances of fatality have been known to result from these causes, but of the pig they seem to have the greatest fear, for the instant the pig approaches, they lay perfectly quiet; he puts his fore paw on their head and soon devours them; many other snakes have a great dread of the swinish family. The rattlesnake herb is said to be an effectual antidote against the effects of their poison, if applied immediately after the wound is given, and that the rattlesnake shows the greatest abhorrence when approaching this herb. The rattlesnake is of a dark brown color, the head is broad and flat, the eyes large and very prominent, and when in vigor are particularly bright; they have a hooked tooth or fang at each side of the mouth, this tooth is hollow, and acts as a tube for the conveyance of the deadly liquid, which is contained in a small bag at the root of this fang, in its under jaw. The received notion, respecting this animal, is, that they acquire an additional rattle every year ; these rattles are like so many ivory rings, and when shaken they make a clattering kind of noise ; the rattlesnake is incapable of making a spring of any distance ; it is said that when these snakes are lying on the ground, that the dazzling brightness of their eyes proves an irresistable charm, and causes birds to drop instinctively when flying.

Spotted snake : the spotted snake is common in all parts of Canada ; it is about three feet long, with a dingy white skin covered with large black spots ; this little reptile, though free from venemous qualities, is nevertheless given to thievish propensities, and will devour young chickens, &c.

The common garter snake is also to be seen in all parts of the provinces, some of them are rather large ; they are marked with black, yellow and white stripes ; they frequent the parts near the dwellings, into which they sometimes approach ; though quite harmless, they will, when irritated, completely change their color, and from being striped become perfectly spotted, and swell out nearly twice their usual size.

Green snake : this is in color a perfect pea-green ; very small, with a remarkably small head ; it is not more than sixteen inches long; it is a handsome little harmless creature.

Yellow snake: this is still a smaller snake than the last, and equally harmless.

Black water snake, which is common in all the lakes and rivers in Upper Canada; some of them are very large and are said to be venomous, but which is very doubtful; the following is an instance which may be considered pretty conclusive that they are not. A boy went to a river for water, he soon came running back with something tightly grasped in his hands, saying he had caught a fine eel, it was a water snake, and although the boy squeezed it tightly to hold it, and kept it in his hands for some time, the animal never attempted to bite him, which seems a good proof that they are not venomous.

Of turtle, there are three or four different kinds; the most common is the small land turtle, inhabiting the borders of the rivers and ponds; they are handsome little creatures; in sun shine and hot days they are seen sitting in rows by the water side, into which they immediately plunge when approached; it is said they are exceeding good eating.

FINIS.

CPSIA information can be obtained
at www.ICGtesting.com
Printed in the USA
LVHW020131010322
712298LV00004B/96